Insight into a Career in Pharmaceutical Sales

Fifth Edition

By Anne Clayton

pharmaceuticalsales.com
655 Deerfield Road
Suite 100-262
Deerfield, IL 60015

International Standard Book Number (ISBN)
ISBN 0-9665121-4-6, Fifth Edition, Published 2003

Previous Editions
ISBN 0-9665121-5-4 Fourth Edition, Published 2002, Out of Print
ISBN 0-9665121-2-X Third Edition, Published 2001, Out of Print
ISBN 0-9665121-1-1 Second Edition, Published 1999, Out of Print
ISBN 0-9665121-0-3 First Edition, Published 1998, Out of Print

Library of Congress Cataloging-in Publication Data
Insight into a Career in Pharmaceutical Sales/Marketing Essentials Incorporated
76-2-4K

Contributing Editors
Victoria R. Tarrani (viki@pacbell.net)
C. B. Stevens (CBSSecMan@aol.com)

This pharmaceuticalsales.com publication is available
to businesses, universities, and organizations
at a special discount when ordered in large quantities.
For more information, contact:
pharmaceuticalsales.com
655 Deerfield Road
Suite 100-262
Deerfield, IL 60015
or on the Internet at www.pharmaceuticalsales.com

Published in the United States of America
Printed in the United States of America

To our readers:

Anne Clayton and other contributors have provided
you with an excellent resource for marketing yourself
and building a career in the pharmaceutical industry.
As you pursue this profession, feel free
to contact us through our web site.
http://www.pharmaceuticalsales.com

pharmaceuticalsales.com
655 Deerfield Road
Suite 100-262
Deerfield, IL 60015

Table of Contents

Introduction

Your Mission

Congratulations! You have just chosen pharmaceuticalsales.com for first-hand insight and career guidance into the pharmaceutical industry. You have taken an important step toward a vital and challenging profession, and are about to embark on a step-by-step journey to a professional career. The pharmaceutical industry is one of the most sought after jobs in sales and marketing professions. This industry has consistently shown exceptional growth over many years and promises to continue as one of the greatest industries of the century. The ever challenging, ever-changing health care market will provide the dedicated individual with professional, business, and personal satisfaction over the course of a life-long career. Again, congratulations, and welcome to your future!

Think of yourself as starting on an exciting mission. You can see the end-point quite clearly. You see yourself enjoying and excelling in a challenging, respected career. You are the consummate sales professional in one of the most prosperous industries in America. You are making a great salary, plus bonus, a company car, and have plenty of benefits! However, you are not exactly sure how to get there from wherever you are now. You have the desire, but need a little push in the right direction.

That is where pharmaceuticalsales.com comes in! Our mission is simple: provide job candidates seeking entry-level sales representative positions in the pharmaceutical industry--like you--with the necessary tools to succeed. That's it! Reading, learning, and applying the lessons in this book provides you with an "insiders" guide to the course of action for greatest success. By practicing the simple down-to-earth steps, you will land the job of your dreams and thereby launch yourself into a highly rewarding and highly compensated life-long professional career.

Insight into a Career in Pharmaceutical Sales (*Insight*, for short) will support you through the important steps. *Insight* provides pertinent industry knowledge, key-networking strategies, essential interviewing preparations, and critical organizational tools that empower you to excel in today's competitive job-hunting environment. In addition, we will do this from the inside perspective by sharing many years of pharmaceutical industry experience and special insights that can only come from being there. The guidance you receive from *Insight* is the combined results of substantial professional involvement in many facets of the sales and marketing of pharmaceutical products, including, and perhaps most importantly, sales management.

Many hours were spent researching, designing, and developing *Insight*. The strategies and tools revealed in this guide were developed from first-hand personal interviews and focus groups. Additionally, we address the career requirements based on many years of experience with professional sales representatives, district sales managers, sales training managers, marketing managers, and regional sales directors, within the pharmaceutical business.

We also have compiled information on specific pharmaceutical companies into a convenient reference (Appendix). Pharmaceuticalsales.com utilizes published sources, such as industry periodicals, annual reports, quarterly 10K filings with the Securities and Exchange Commission, personal interviews, and other such resources to answer your questions and guide you to a rewarding career. The information in *Insight* reflects current and historical research, and can be used as an entree into the industry.

Chapter 1 gives you an overview of this dynamic business. **The Future of the Pharmaceutical Industry** includes history, current issues, and the outlook of this very important industry.

In Chapter 2, **The Sales Representative,** *Insight* gives you an in-depth view of today's pharmaceutical representative. You will see typical compensation packages, various job descriptions, career advancement, and positive and negative aspects of the position.

Chapter 3, **Best Foot Forward,** discloses that, although no resume will win you employment, many common mistakes will quickly eliminate you from the process. You will learn the twenty simple rules for resumes and cover letters.

Preparation is the backbone of your job-hunting endeavor. Understanding your target market is perhaps the most important step in securing the perfect job. How to gather and compile this relevant research is outlined in Chapter 4, **Vital Research.**

In Chapter 5, **Networking News,** *Insight* discloses our unique way to show you how to market yourself within the industry. This is key to successful employment. All avenues to reach this goal are explained through each stage of your process.

Now it is time to advance your career in the pharmaceuticalsales.com way. Chapter 6, **The Interview,** shows you the way by providing insight into successful interviewing strategies. It focuses on the most frequently asked questions and suggests ways to tailor your responses in order to maximize your impact with every answer. Today the most common first dialogue is via the telephone. Present yourself well and you will enter phase two--first, second, and final interviews with corporate executives. The possibilities are discussed with reference to what behavioral characteristics companies are seeking. Also included is a list of guidelines for professional attire that is imperative for outstanding presentations.

Now that you have that great interview set up, what do you say? Chapter 7, **Your Questions,** provides questions that complement you as a candidate, and generate information that you need to win the job. This chapter also shows you the most intelligent way to turn the tables and take control of the interview.

There are three outcomes from every interview process. Chapter 8, **Decisions, Decisions,** reveals how to handle each situation with the composure that insures positive results.

The Conclusion emphasizes **Your Commitment** to this career choice. It focuses on the continuous implementation of the tools you acquired through *Insight*. The knowledge and skills contained in this guide will work for you to maximize your potential for professional employment in this rewarding and dynamic industry.

The Appendix contains 35 Company Profiles that offer a comprehensive reference to today's largest pharmaceutical companies and contract sales organizations (CSO's). This is a convenient resource designed to help you organize your newly acquired information and document your networking contacts for future interviews. The Appendix also includes several worksheets which provide a means to record your progress, document the details of your job search, and organize your growing network of contacts in the pharmaceutical companies.

Chapter 1
The New Golden Age: The Future of the Pharmaceutical Industry

The pharmaceutical industry is among the largest, most stable, and fastest growing of all businesses in the United States. It was only a few years ago that discussions concerning national price controls weighed heavily on the industry and its investors. However, Wall Street's worries were unnecessary. According to *IMS Health* (the foremost provider of global marketing research in this industry), North America (U.S. and Canada) remains the largest market by far, representing 50 percent of the total worldwide sales in 2001. North America is not only the largest but also the fastest growing pharmaceutical market in the world, with sales up 17 percent in 2001 and another 13 percent in 2002 to a total of $152 billion. U.S. drug sales are expected to increase at an annual rate of about 12 percent through 2005.

Based on Standard & Poor's (S & P) Industry Surveys, global sales of pharmaceuticals were up 8.5 percent to $395 billion in 2002. This includes both prescription (ethical) and over-the-counter (OTC) drugs. *PhRMA* estimates that the percentage of total sales by U.S. companies in global markets is 35 percent and growing. The strongest competitive foreign markets are Europe and Japan, followed by Asia, Africa, Australia and Latin America. This booming global market provides opportunity in long-term sales careers and the possibility of international travel.

Pharmaceutical manufacturing is an almost recession proof business, and it remains somewhat insulated from economic cycles that affect other commercial endeavors. *Fortune* magazine's yearly survey shows that CEO's award the "most highly respected" rating on a consistent basis to Pharmaceutical Sales Organizations. Investors will continue to make funds available for Research and Development (R&D), and more salespeople will be needed. This means job security, promotions, and competitive compensation packages.

Despite a long and successful record of accomplishment, the pharmaceutical industry is not immune to change. Major shifts are taking place that constitute both threats to and opportunities for drug companies. The healthcare system is in flux due to the pressures of cost, managed care, consolidations, vertical integrations among corporations that produce drugs, doctor recommendations, and patients who purchase the products. As the clientele becomes more knowledgeable and powerful, their demands increase and they take charge of their own health care. Rapidly changing demographics create new markets. Many new drugs carry patents that are in effect for a shorter timeframe, and existing patents on 42 major drugs are expiring in the next five years. Salespeople must adapt well to change and remain well educated about the company and the products they represent in order to succeed in their careers.

Several positive changes in the pharmaceutical industry include corporate mergers, vertical integration, alliances, and outsourcing within the industry. Mergers have given rise to larger, more secure companies with greater economies of scale. Alliances have grown the capabilities for research and development ensuring the flow of new drugs. Outsourcing has given rise to contract sales organizations (CSO) in providing an effective way to employ a large sales force. CSOs will be discussed in later chapters of this book.

The future is bright and demands qualified salespeople. The market for pharmaceuticals will generate a 6 to 7 percent annual growth in worldwide sales over the next five years and beyond. In fact, prescription drug spending will double in the next five years, according to *Merck-Medco Managed Care LLC's* 2001 drug trend report. The forces that will increase the demand are listed below. Each of these will be discussed in the remainder of this chapter:

* The aging global population and increasing life expectancies.
* Successful industry track record on Wall Street.
* Increased investments in R&D and a constant flow of new drugs.
* Innovation and advances in technology.
* New markets for pharmaceuticals.
* Demand for cost-effective health care.
* Possibility for Medicare drug coverage.
* Identifying and treating overlooked patient populations.
* A high demand for better lifestyle and improved quality of life.
* Shorter FDA approval times and relaxed marketing restrictions.
* Expanding promotional spending and consumer oriented marketing.
* Educated health-conscious consumers.
* Industry giants, growth companies, and blockbuster drugs.

THE AGING GLOBAL POPULATION AND INCREASING LIFE EXPECTANCIES

The two most powerful demographic trends are the aging population and increased life expectancies. These two factors are generating growth demands for pharmaceuticals as both dramatically increase the number of elderly persons. The over-65 population in the U.S. is expected to expand by about 31 percent from 2001 through 2015, according to the U.S. Census Bureau. Every day more than 6,000 Americans celebrate their 65th birthdays. This phenomenon is a reflection of the baby boomer generation. Aging will provide a tremendous marketing opportunity for prescription drugs. A global study by The World Health Organization shows that this older population will increase from the current level of 380 million to over 800 million by 2025.

At the turn of the 19th century, the average life expectancy was only 47 years. A child born today can expect to live to be almost 80. These longer life spans are due to advances in medical care, improved standards of living, and the development of innovative medications and vaccines to treat deadly diseases such as polio, diphtheria, heart disease, and the various forms of cancer.

As more people live longer, they will naturally experience an increase in health problems due simply to aging. Additionally, the long-term effects of unhealthy habits such as smoking, obesity, poor diet, and lack of exercise result in increased incidence of diseases. Thus, the over-65 population becomes candidates for various treatments including increased ethical and OTC drugs. On the average, the elderly consume three times more prescription medications than persons under the age 65 do.

Major problem conditions in the elderly are heart disease, stroke, arthritis, cancers, depression, impotence, osteoporosis, Parkinson's, and Alzheimer's disease. Pharmaceuticals targeting these diseases will be in greater demand. The industry will dedicate the majority of its massive $30.5 billion annual R&D spending over the coming years toward the development of new treatments for these health problems.

SUCCESSFUL INDUSTRY TRACK RECORD ON WALL STREET

The pharmaceutical industry is considerably insulated from changes in the economic climate. Simply put, people will always be sick and will always require medications regardless of the economy. Drug pricing inelasticity indicates that patients will buy a needed prescription despite the price. If an alternate medication is available, but not as effective, the more costly product will still be purchased. For many patients, insurance affects the price of the medication by requiring a small co-pay or expenditure, which usually means that price is not an issue.

Historically, this business has provided excellent growth for investors. The stock market recorded unparalleled growth in the 1980's and 1990's. Operating profit margins (earnings as a percentage of sales) have come down in recent years due to reduced pricing flexibility, but the industry average still exceeds 30 percent--more than twice that of the typical corporation in the S & P Industrial Index. The drug industry pretax and net income returns are substantially higher than in other industries. The net earnings as a percentage of sales averaged 15.7 percent for the five-year period through 2001, compared with 5.7 percent for general industry. Return on equity (ROE), or net earnings, as a percentage of average stockholders' equity, is approximately 25 percent--ranking pharmaceuticals among the highest of all industries. The ROE reflects the impressive profit margins.

This industry has come under fire in past years from claims that its profits are greater than necessary to provide a return on investment in research and development. The fact is, in financial terms, drug manufacturing is a high-risk business. For every 5,000 compounds discovered, only one ever reaches the market. Of those, less than one third will sell enough to recoup their R&D costs. However, when a newly marketed drug is widely successful, the sales on that product can be in the billions of dollars. This is the primary reason for the industry's high profit margins. Continued growth depends on private investors having the confidence that they will receive a competitive return on their investment that is commensurate with the risk. A June 1994 study by the Congressional Budget Office (CBO) found that measures of industry profitability do not take into account the inherent riskiness of pharmaceutical R&D.

INCREASED INVESTMENTS IN R&D AND A CONSTANT FLOW OF NEW DRUGS

Today's top corporations are research and development driven. New products are the lifeblood of the industry. Research-based pharmaceutical companies invested $30.5 billion in R&D in 2001, an 18.5 percent increase over 2000 and more than triple the 1990 level. These expenditures include $23.6 billion spent within the United States by both U.S.-owned and foreign-owned firms, plus an additional $6.8 billion spent abroad by U.S.-owned firms *(figure 1)*. These organizations have more than tripled their R&D expenditures since 1990.

FIGURE 1:   PRESCRIPTION PHARMACEUTICAL R&D EXPENDITURES AT RESEARCH-BASED PHARMACEUTICAL COMPANIES, IN BILLIONS OF DOLLARS

Source: Pharmaceutical Research & Manufactures Association

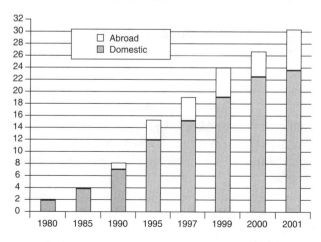

Over the past 20 years, the percentage of sales allocated to R&D has increased from 11.4 percent in 1970 to 18.5 percent in 2001. Meanwhile, the average R&D-to-sales ratio for other U.S. industries is less than 4 percent. Based on corporate tax data compiled by Standard & Poor's *Compustat,* pharmaceutical manufacturers invest a higher percentage of sales in R&D than any other industry, including high-tech electronics, aerospace, automobile, and office equipment such as computers, printers, and peripheral devices. The nature of the drug industry requires the most intensive R&D structures in the U.S. economy. R&D spending is rising sharply, both in dollar terms and as a percentage of total sales; it has doubled every five years since 1970.

The United States industry is the world leader, and invents about 70% of the world's new medical therapies. Of the 100 most widely prescribed drugs, 94 were discovered with private funds without any government support. However, publicly funded health research has also increased substantially in recent years. Government and academic scientists lead the way in basic research about diseases. Then drug industry scientists translate these academic advances into medications to prevent, cure, and treat the diseases.

Drug development time and cost has grown dramatically as science has allowed researchers to target more complicated diseases and test more complex drug molecules. The average number of clinical trials (drug testing for effectiveness in humans) conducted before FDA approval has more than doubled since 1980. The time to bring a newly discovered compound to market is between 10 and 15 years. The average cost of developing a drug is more that $802 million in 2002, according to Tufts Center for the Study of Drug Development. Though the average patent life after FDA approval is 10 years, only 3 out of 10 approved drugs recover R&D costs. Companies must rely on highly successful products to fund R&D and maintain a constant flow of many new drugs in order to remain profitable and competitive.

An estimated 50,000 pharmaceutical scientists are currently researching more than 1,000 new medicines in twelve major drug categories. These categories represent the major causes of disease and death in this country, and require the highest outlay of healthcare costs. Close to 320 anticancer drugs are in the pipeline, 187 drugs and vaccines for children, over 130 AIDS treatments, 100 for heart disease and strokes, 85 for mental health, and 30 for arthritis. This proliferation should keep both the industry and the public healthy for many years to come.

INNOVATION AND ADVANCES IN TECHNOLOGY

There is also a constant demand from the consumer for quality health care. Americans have come to expect the best and latest in health care technology.

In the past, valuable discoveries were often made by accident. The twenty-first century, however, brings sweeping changes in biomedical and pharmaceutical industries. The U.S. Human Genome Project unlocked the mystery of DNA. By completing the map of the human genome, researchers will be able to design medicines for specific patient populations. This will result in a future that provides medications tailored to an individual's genetic makeup. Physicians will be able to treat and prevent the root causes of cancer, heart and arthritic conditions, and Alzheimer disease. New products will combat illnesses that were once considered the inevitable consequences of old age: frailty, vision failure, sexual dysfunction, and loss of mental acuity.

Most of the top corporations are aligning with genomic companies or have established genomic research facilities of their own. Pharmaceutical companies using scientific data from genome research will gain a significant competitive advantage. This advantage, according to industry analysts, will not prove profitable in the near or medium term, but could potentially take the form of a rich research and development pipeline leading to highly effective and lucrative medicines in the next decade.

The biotechnology industry is having an impact on medicine right now. It is on the forefront of innovation and high technology resulting in new discoveries every day. These "biotech" companies, specializing in genetically altered drugs, gene research, and molecular biology will provide new therapies and also improved therapies over existing problems.

New corporate marriages between biotechnology companies and pharmaceutical concerns are common. This practice provides small, innovative biotech companies with the financial backing for research, plus management and marketing efforts to successfully launch new products into the marketplace.

NEW MARKETS FOR PHARMACEUTICALS

Recent events in major markets around the world are opening tremendous growth opportunities for today's global pharmaceutical corporations. The "Third World" is becoming more developed economically. Rising standards of living in Latin America, Asia, Africa, and Eastern Europe are also good news for U.S. companies. As emerging nations raise the economic standing of the population, one of their top priorities is to improve healthcare. An increased demand for medications to provide better healthcare in many countries equates to a longer life expectancy for their residents.

The forecast calls for an explosion of growth in developing countries over the next five years, and in specific pharmaceuticals to aid the global aging population. The world pharmaceutical market grows 8 percent annually, reaching a total value of $406 billion in 2002 (source: *IMS Health*). The North American, European, Japanese, and Latin American markets will continue to dominate, accounting for 92 percent of all global sales during that time *(figure 3)*. Globally, the Middle East, Australia, Southeast Asia, and China are expected to grow most quickly. In Europe, Poland has the fastest growth rate, followed by Sweden, the Czech Republic, and Ireland.

The top three U.S. companies in global sales, based on *IMS Health* data, are Novartis, Merck, and GlaxoSmithKline. The fastest growing companies for the same year were Pfizer and Eli Lilly. China, with over one billion people, is a major potential market. According to S & P's *Industry Surveys*, major U.S. companies doing business in both Russia and China include Johnson & Johnson, Merck, Bristol-Myers Squibb, Eli Lilly, and Schering-Plough. The pharmaceutical industry provides excellent opportunities for career advancement in sales and marketing to various global markets. Adding to the potential for global pharmaceutical sales and marketing careers is the fact that many of the major U.S. companies are divisions or subsidiaries of large parent companies based primarily in Europe or Japan.

FIGURE 3: World Pharmaceutical Markets
Source: Standard & Poor's Industry Survey

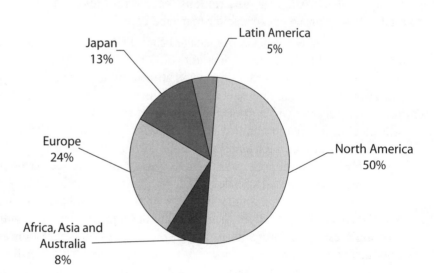

There is an inherent risk in global markets. Economies can be unstable, shaped by politics and world events. Recent problems in Russia, Eastern Europe, Afghanistan, England, the United States, and other countries may cause more U.S. drug companies to lose money in their total global portfolios. However, health is a growing global concern. Moreover, the threat of bioterrorism presents challenges and opportunities for the industry.

DEMAND FOR COST-EFFECTIVE HEALTH CARE

Prescription drug therapy is cost-effective. This means that a treatment or medication meets a specified goal at an acceptable cost compared to surgery, hospitalization, physician visits, and nursing care. Pharmaceuticals often eliminate the need for these more expensive interventions. For example, prescription drug therapy for ulcers costs $1,000 per year, but replaces the need for ulcer surgery costing $25,000. Nearly $400 billion would be saved by taking advantage of more cost effective medicinal treatments and cures for the seven major uncured diseases (Cardiovascular, Cancer, Alzheimer's, Diabetes, Arthritis, Depression, Stroke, Osteoporosis). Nearly 300 medicines are in development for these diseases.

The expense of caring for patients with migraine headaches is being lowered primarily by one drug. The expenditures for this drug increased dramatically, but the costs of treating migraines declined 41 percent because of treatment with the medicine. These costs include health care, lost time at work, lost wages, etc. Using this particular therapy for treating migraines, one study showed that this drug saved employers $435 per month per employee due to a reduction in lost productivity on the job.

However, the current system of healthcare delivery can be inefficient, and this has given rise to "managed care." Eliminating inefficiencies in the system is the goal of managed care organizations (MCO's), such as health maintenance organizations (HMO's) and pharmacy benefit management companies (PBM's). These organizations manage the pharmaceutical benefit for large employers, hospitals, nursing homes, and other clients at relatively lower cost. They insist on the use of lower cost generics whenever possible and have established formularies, or lists of preferred drugs approved for reimbursement. Although prescriptions account for only 15 percent of the MCO's medical costs, they are the fastest growing expense for managed care.

Essentially offshoots of managed care, PBM companies function as intermediaries between pharmaceutical manufacturers and large drug purchasers. They also provide other services such as claims processing, mail order pharmacy, utilization management, and physician monitoring and education. PBM's can represent millions of members, or "covered lives" and wield broad decision-making power over which drugs their members can buy. These members give PBM's a powerful influence against pharmaceutical manufacturers. They are able to negotiate discounts or rebates from a manufacturer in return for increasing usage of the manufacturer's product. These rebates can be passed along by way of lower premiums to the employer and lower co-payments for the patient. Managed care has become the biggest domestic market for pharmaceuticals. *IMS Health* conducted a study and discovered that MCO's accounted for 71% of all U.S. retail prescriptions issued during 2001 (see *figure 4*). The growth of managed care has a positive impact on the pharmaceutical industry by covering prescription drugs for its members. Drug coverage by a third party, such as managed care, or other insurance companies, removes or minimizes price as a factor for the individual who seeks medical care and ultimately fills a prescription at the pharmacy. In fact, the dominance of third party payment is one of the primary forces behind the increasing number of prescriptions being written and dispensed.

A growing tool for managing drug costs by managed care is the "three-tiered co-pay" pricing system. Under this system, generic drugs have the lowest co-payments, preferred drugs listed on the HMO's formulary require a higher co-payment, and brand drugs not on the formulary require the highest out-of-pocket payment. According to Scott-Levin, a market research firm, about 40% of all HMO covered lives are enrolled in three-tier plans. Managed Care pharmacy costs climbed by 12% in 2000, slightly down from the 15% rise in 1999, a decrease that is attributed to the three-tiered co-pay.

FIGURE 4: MANAGED CARE TRENDS -- PERCENTAGE OF TOTAL PRESCRIPTIONS BY PAYER TYPE
Source: **IMS HEALTH**

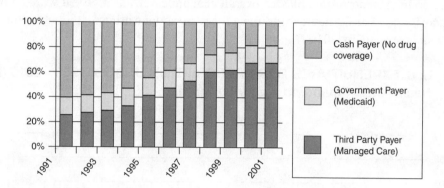

Automated mail order processing using sophisticated computer technology to handle large volumes of prescriptions is one of the PBM's strongest tools. Through economies of scale, a PBM can sell drugs by mail at lower prices than retail pharmacies can.

Managed care continues to grow. Based on data provided by *IMS Health*, persons covered by managed care plans accounted for 71 percent of all prescriptions dispensed in the U.S. in 2001. This compares with 60 percent in 1997, and about 65 percent in 1998. An estimated 115 million Americans are enrolled in drug benefits managed by PBM's, or close to 75 percent of all employed persons.

Total health care spending in the U.S. increased 8.7 percent in 2001 reaching $1.4 trillion, according to a review conducted by the federal government. This is the greatest rate of increase than any of the previous ten years. With the focus on containing healthcare costs, there has been a popular notion that hospitals, physicians, and pharmaceutical companies have benefited from increased pricing. It is also a popular notion that the culprit in the high cost of healthcare is the high cost of medicines, and that

FIGURE 5: U.S. NATIONAL HEALTH CARE EXPENDITURES, 2001
Source: Health Care Financing Administration

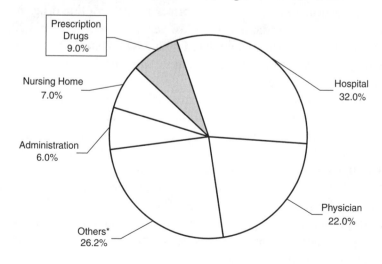

*Includes non-physician professional services, non-durables, over-the-counter medication, public health activities, construction, net cost of private insurance.

Americans are spending more on prescription drugs than on other health care items or services. This is a false assumption. In fact, prescription drug spending is a small fraction of the total costs. It is estimated that expenditures for prescription pharmaceuticals made up only 9 percent of the health-care bill in the United States in 2001 *(figure 5)*. This is an increase from 6 percent in 1998 and 7.9 in 1999. This rise is due to increased pre-scription utilization, and remains a small percentage of the total healthcare cost. However, the percentage of healthcare cost attributed to pharmaceuticals is projected to increase over the next several years reaching 11.4 percent in 2005 and 13.9 percent in 2010. That is due to a predicted jump in pharmaceutical spending of 16-17 percent annually over the next two years and then slowing to 10 percent annually through 2010. The lower rate of increase is predicted due to health plans and private insurance payers becoming more restrictive, and health insurance premiums increasing, plus an overall economic downturn. Even with the projected lower rate of increase, total healthcare expenditures for prescriptions drugs will double from 1999 to 2005 and nearly double again by 2010 *(figure 6)*.

FIGURE 6:   U. S. EXPENDITURES FOR PRESCRIPTION DRUGS: 1980 - 2010 (BILLIONS)
Source: Health Care Financing Administration.

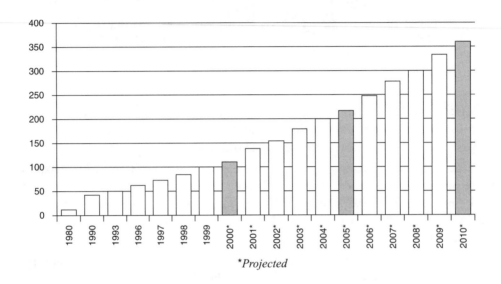

*Projected

The money spent on drugs, questions of pricing, and insurance coverage of prescriptions will continue to draw the critical attention of politicians and the media. Most discussions on the role of pharmaceuticals in the health care system focus, not on their long-term value, but on their short-term cost. One reason for this is that drug purchases are one of the few health care expenses paid directly out of pocket, especially for the elderly who do not have drug coverage under Medicare. Despite all the measures implemented by government and private third-party payers, prices for prescription drugs have continued to increase by a wider margin than general inflation. In the 10 years between 1990 and 2000, prescription prices increased at an annual rate of 4.6 percent compared with 2.8 percent for the Consumer Price Index (CPI). Following several years of relative pricing stability, prescription prices moved notably higher in 2001 in both the branded and generic sectors of the market. Based on data from the Bureau of Labor Statistics, drug prices rose 6 percent, compared with a 1.6 percent rise in the CPI. In addition to price increases, overall increasing demand also influences spending for pharmaceuticals--more people are filling prescriptions now than in the past. To illustrate, U.S. total health-care spending rose 8.7 percent in 2001, the greatest increase in 10 years. In the same year, U.S. prescription drug spending increased 16.9 percent. Again, it is both the demand for prescription drugs and higher drug prices that are fueling growth. According to IMS, only 4.9 percentage points out of the 16.9 percent increase resulted from increased prices. Of the remaining 12 percent increase, 8.7 resulted from a higher volume of prescriptions dispensed, and 3.3 percent from the introduction of new medicines *(figure 7)*. Historically the use of pharmaceutical products has been lamented, rather than applauded regardless of the improvements they bring to healthcare.

FIRURE: 7 **PRESCRIPTION PHARMACEUTICAL SALES GROWTH RATE, INCREASING DUE TO VOLUME NOT PRICE, U.S. MARKET.**

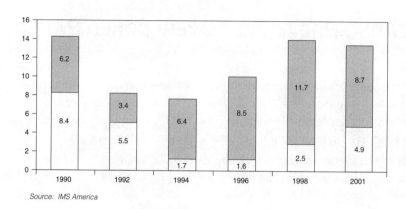

Source: IMS America

Growing evidence supports the assertion that increased use of innovative medications can help people avoid more expensive and invasive treatments. In other words, pharmaceuticals are slowly being recognized as the most cost-effective method of treating many conditions. Scientific evaluation and education acknowledges that medications protect the quality of care and control the costs. Therefore, not only would more spending on drugs make and keep more people well, it would shrink the overall cost of care. No one is more interested in the overall cost of care than MCO's. Many MCO's have initiated "care management" or "disease management" programs for patients with chronic diseases, many of which rely heavily on prescription medications and increased drug utilization. The purpose of these programs is to control costs associated with treating chronic illness and improving the quality of care. So it follows that with intensified focus on disease management by managed care and with increasing numbers enrolling in managed care, we will see more drug utilization. As managed care grows, so will the demand for cost-effective ways to treat diseases--and that means greater demand for pharmaceuticals. The development of innovative pharmaceuticals is the most promising and cost-effective method to keep Americans out of hospitals, out of operating rooms, and out of nursing homes. In short, pharmaceuticals help keep people healthy and productive.

MEDICARE DRUG COVERAGE

Another factor that may significantly increase demand for pharmaceuticals is the implementation of drug coverage for all senior citizens under the Medicare program. Medicare is the federal program that pays healthcare expenses for 40 million of the elderly population in the U.S. While Medicare currently pays for most medical and hospital services, it does not cover outpatient prescription medications. Thus, the elderly will either pay cash, purchase supplemental insurance to cover prescriptions, or rely on existing retirement benefits, which often include ongoing prescription benefits. This issue received much attention during the 2002 congressional election and is a major focus of the current administration. Details of a program are presented in President Bush's fiscal 2004 budget. One problem holding up progress is the difference in Congress between Democrats and Republicans on how the plan should be structured. The argument runs along typical party lines of conservative (less government) and liberal (more government) approaches. Republicans favor a plan run by private companies such as existing MCO's and the role of government is simply to pay for it. Democrats desire the creation of a comprehensive federal bureaucracy that would directly provide drug benefits. The Democratic plan could cost $500 billion over ten years and put the government in a powerful position as the largest purchaser of prescription drugs. While pharmaceutical companies would benefit from the large increase in product demand, they fear that the plan would carry with it the 30-40 percent price discounting that exists in other government-run drug coverage programs such as state Medicaid, Tricare, Champus, and the Veterans Administration.

To alleviate pressure on Medicare enrollees due to price concerns, seven major drug companies recently launched a discount card for prescription purchases by low-income senior citizens, called the "Together Rx Card." In what Secretary of Health and Human Services, Tommy Thompson, called a "tremendous new initiative," the new card entitles Medicare beneficiaries to price discounts of 20 to 40 percent on more than 150 popular prescription drugs.

IDENTIFYING AND TREATING PREVIOUSLY OVERLOOKED PATIENT POPULATIONS

We are in an age of ever expanding knowledge, technological advances, and new scientific and medical discoveries. Our knowledge of the human body, the processes of disease, and our genetic makeup will be translated into new capabilities to study, diagnose, and treat a variety of illnesses. Even in a time of recession, we are also in an age of an expanding access to the healthcare system.

The methods and extent to which common diseases can be detected is improving. More sophisticated, sensitive, and less expensive diagnostic technologies are leading to widespread use of screening programs, which lead to better analysis. Thus, diagnosis and treatment for common diseases such as elevated cholesterol, osteoporosis, and prostate cancer can be addressed at the onset.

DEMAND FOR "LIFESTYLE" OR "QUALITY OF LIFE" PHARMACEUTICALS

More than ever, people want pharmaceuticals to enhance their lives, not simply treat illnesses. Generally, the baby boomer generation is not staying healthy by exercising, eating well and getting enough sleep, but rather by aggressively pursuing medical care when--and even before--health problems arise. Their expectations are that modern healthcare should fix their medical problems. This led to the "new drug culture"--the concept of drug products that will improve a person's functional capacity and overall well being. Baby boomers are attracted to "better-for-you" products, which has created greater demand for new pharmaceuticals.

Our high speed, stressful lifestyle is feeding this frenzy. People often continue their lifestyle of poor diets, lack of exercise, and no stress management. These unhealthy habits are well-known risk factors for many common diseases such as ulcers, depression, obesity, and impotence. The four largest therapy classes in the world can be linked to unhealthy lifestyles--they are, in the order of global sales: Antiulcerants, Cholesterol Reducers, Antidepressants, and Antihypertensives. These drug categories treat conditions that have been described as "diseases of civilization" because they are a largely a phenomenon of Western culture.

Another growing therapy class is the treatment of erectile dysfunction. Weight management is also a rapidly growing therapeutic category. These therapies give rise to questions about what should or should not be considered a medical problem or a disease, and more importantly raise the questions of who should pay for their treatment. That definition may be expanding to include problems that can be treated with "quality of life" and "lifestyle" medications. Examples of such problems include the appearance of wrinkles and loss of hair.

FDA APPROVAL TIMES AND MARKETING RESTRICTIONS

As the principal federal agency responsible for enforcing U.S. drug laws, the Food and Drug Administration (FDA) regulates the introduction of new drugs. Pharmaceutical companies must submit extensive data to the FDA demonstrating both the safety and the effectiveness of new drugs before receiving approval for sale in the U.S. In addition, the FDA requires that drugs be produced according to specified "good manufacturing practices" (GMP) guidelines. Manufacturing plants are subject to FDA approval and must be inspected periodically. Once a product is approved, the manufacturer must also receive FDA authorization for its marketing practices. In other words, the FDA must approve what the pharmaceutical companies can say about their products, as well as how they go about publicizing them. The claims that Pharmaceutical Sales Representatives make to physicians must meet FDA standards.

Pharmaceutical companies until recently were benefiting from a friendlier regulatory environment for new drugs. To help bring down the high cost of drug development, the FDA began streamlining the review process in 1992. The average review time for a newly introduced drug is now 12-18 months, down from 35 months in 1996. Current drug approvals had almost doubled from an average of only 70 each year from 1990 to 1994. However, the FDA appears to have taken a stricter approach to the drug industry. The number of new drugs approved declined in 2000 through 2002, while the time it took to approve them increased. There is good news for 2003 in that, according to a report by Lehman Brothers, there will be a modest rise in new drug approvals to at least 30 novel drugs, up from 25 in 2002. The analysts estimated that, in terms of product value, the sales potential of drugs likely to be approved in 2003 is $21 billion; the corresponding figure for 2002 was $18 billion.

The FDA issues marketing guidelines which regulate how pharmaceutical companies promote their products. Marketing guidelines have become less restrictive in recent years. For example, restrictions on direct-to-consumer (DTC) advertising, particularly via the television, have been lifted. This contributed to an increase in DTC advertising by pharmaceutical companies, leading more patients to make specific requests for brand-name products to their physicians. Another restriction that has been eased is the limitation on discussions by Sales Representatives concerning "off-label" or unapproved uses of their products. This means that companies can expand the types of patients or diseases that their existing products can be prescribed to treat.

EXPANDING PROMOTIONAL SPENDING AND CONSUMER ORIENTED MARKETING

Pharmaceutical companies have stepped up marketing efforts on all fronts to take advantage of favorable conditions in the market. Money spent by pharmaceutical companies for research and development was $30.5 billion in 2001; promotional spending was $8.6 billion in the same year (IMS Health). Sampling costs were valued at $10.5 billion, according to Med Ad News. These three costs alone--R&D, promotional spending and sampling--consume nearly half of pharmaceutical sales revenue. See *figure 8* for the break down in promotional spending for 2001.

Typically, sales and marketing of prescription drugs fall into two main categories--professional promotions and direct to consumer advertising (DTC). Professional promotion includes: sales presentations in doctors' offices, hospitals and pharmacies; medical journal advertising; drug samples; meetings and events including continuing medical education (CME); direct mail; Internet-based programs; and promotional items (pens, pads, office trinkets). The various strategies in the promotional mix are changing as DTC and Internet-based promotions expand. However, the overall strategy continues to be spearheaded by large sales forces of professional Pharmaceutical Representatives.

FIGURE 8:   PROMOTIONAL SPENDING FOR YEAR 2001
Sources: *IMS, Scott Levin*

Doctor Office Promotion (includes sales force)	$4.8 billion
Hospital Promotion (includes sales force)	$760 million
Journal Advertising	$380 million
Direct to Consumer Advertising	$2.7 billion
Sampling	$10.5 billion
Total Promotional Spending Mix	**$19.1 billion**

Direct-to-consumer advertising targets specific groups of customers in print and broadcast media such as television, radio, billboards, magazines, and newspapers. The practice was almost non-existent in the industry until the mid-nineties and has nearly doubled every year since 1994. This growth has been helped by several trends.

1. The FDA has relaxed regulations on DTC advertising.
2. Patients today want to be more involved in their own healthcare so they are more receptive to advertising.
3. The public's medical knowledge is expanding.
4. The public's desire and ability to access the Internet is expanding.
5. Physicians are more willing to comply with patients' requests for drugs seen in DTC ads.

Increased DTC advertising has led to greater consumer recognition of the benefits of pharmaceutical therapies, and created brand recognition and loyalty. This strategy is not always popular among physicians, but such advertising makes more patients aware of ailments and encourages them to see their doctors to learn more. One poll of 1,200 people showed 74 percent believe these ads help them be more involved in their own health care; 67 percent say the ads teach them about risks and benefits of drugs. Of patients who talked to their doctors about a drug that they saw advertised, 50 percent asked for a prescription by name and 70 percent of them received a prescription for the brand they wanted. According to Scott-Levin, a pharmaceutical industry market research firm, there is a direct correlation between the spending on DTC and product sales; those products that are heavily advertised are the ones most often requested by patients.

FIGURE 9:   SPENDING ON DIRECT TO CONSUMER ADVERTISING, IN BILLIONS
Source: IMS, Scott Levin

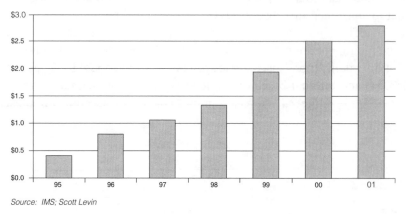

Source: IMS; Scott Levin

DTC is expected to continue to expand at a steady pace in the years ahead. Though television is the dominant medium, companies are increasing their annual budgets for more varied types of DTC advertising. *Figure 9* shows increases in spending for DTC from $400 million in 1995 to $2.8 billion in 2001. *Figure10* presents the top ten prescription drugs leading the industry in DTC spending.

FIGURE 10: TOP 10 SPENDING FOR DIRECT-TO-CONSUMER ADS, IN MILLIONS
Source: **IMS Health/Competitive Media Reporting U.S. Prescription Drugs, 2001.**

Medication	Drug Company	What it treats	DTC Expenditure
Vioxx	Merck & Co.	arthritis and pain	$135
Celebrex	Pharmacia	arthritis and pain	130
Nexium	AstraZeneca	ulcers	127
Viagra	Pfizer	erectile dysfunction	101
Allegra	Aventis	allergies	90
Zocor	Merck & Co.	cholesterol	85
Gluccophage	Bristol-Meyers Squibb	diabetes	82
Clartin	Schering-Plough	allergies	80
Imitrex	GlaxoSmithKline	migrane	71
Flonase	GlaxoSmithKline	allergies	66
Total Top Ten			**$967**

Although the pharmaceutical industry was slow to embrace the Internet as a marketing tool, today virtually every company has a product information web site and some have e-business divisions. According to Cyber Dialogue, a New York-based Internet market research firm, companies spent close to $100 million on Internet marketing, or about 9.65 percent of the total DTC budget. A growing number of pharmaceutical companies are using the Internet to make sales presentations directly to physicians. Some doctors respond to the convenience of logging on to a web site from their office and then speaking with a Pharmaceutical Representative. Early research shows that physicians may be willing to spend more time with the representative when the sales call is conducted on line.

Pharmaceutical Sales Representatives are the industry's most critical tools for promoting its innovative product offering. During the early 1990's, the industry began to cut back on its sales force size. The assumption was that once managed care dominated the healthcare system the physician would no longer be the decision-maker and there would be no need for large forces in the physician offices. However, experience in recent years has shown that even under managed care physicians remained the ultimate decision-makers in choosing prescription medications. Successful companies have returned to traditional "detailing" and sampling strategies, greatly expanding their representative staff in the process. The return on investment is obvious for the physician office-based sales force. Market share increases when you add additional Sales Representatives. Sales forces, including contract Sales Representatives, grew by 15 percent from 1997 to 1998. That trend continues today. In 2000, sales force growth continues at the rate of 16% among the top 40 companies, according to Scott-Levin. In 1995, there were approximately 40,000 Sales Representatives in the U.S. By 2000, there were more than 80,000, as reported by IMS Health. *Figure 11* presents the largest U.S. companies by sales force size.

FIGURE 11:   FIFTEEN LARGEST U.S. SALES FORCES 2001
SOURCE: Includes contract sales forces. Numbers are approximate.

Company Name	Number of Sales Reps
Pfizer, Inc.	8,200
GlaxoSmithKline Plc.	8,000
Merck & Co.	7,000
AstraZeneca, Plc.	6,000
Novartis	5,900
Johnson & Johnson	5,500
Bristol Myers Squibb Co.	5,200
Aventis SA	4,700
Pharmacia Corp.	4,500
Wyeth/American Home Products	4,400
Schering-Plough Corp.	4,400
Eli Lilly & Co.	4,100
Abbott Laboratories	3,200
Sanofi-Synthelabo	2,200
Roche	2,100
Total Top 15	**71,000**

The year 2002 brought a major shift in the pharmaceutical industry's promotional tactics. Led by PhRMA member companies, the industry revised its voluntary guidelines concerning the marketing of drugs to physicians. While this new code still allows treating physicians to reasonably-priced meals, guests who are not part of the medical practice (spouses, for example) would not be allowed to participate. The purpose of the revisions is to keep the sales representatives focused on educating and informing physicians and less focused on business related entertainment. The venue for educating physicians is now mandated to be "conducive to providing scientific or educational information," according to a report by the Associated Press.   Promotional items that are no longer acceptable include, among others, logo-imprinted golf balls, floral arrangements and tickets to sporting events, theater and concerts. There is no mechanism for enforcing the revised code, but companies who participated in the process, as well as other companies, are expected to voluntarily adhere to the guidelines.

Why the change in promotional tactics? Scrutiny by the media and politicians of pharmaceutical promotional practices has been intense. A survey conducted by the Kaiser Family Foundation found that perks from sales representatives such as meals, event tickets and travel were received by 61 percent of the more than 2,600 U.S. physicians polled, and that a substantial portion of the promotional budget of pharmaceutical companies was directed at these activities. The assumption is made that these "perks," rather than physician education activities, are unduly impacting physician prescribing. "We think there are some very valid concerns and as an industry we are looking at ways to address concerns while still continuing the very important work of educating and communicating to physicians information about new products," said Jeff Trewitt, a spokesman for PhRMA. Many sales representatives welcome this change in tactics in order to alleviate the concern over physician gifts, level the playing field among large and small companies and focus on face-to-face physician interaction in daily selling situations.

AN EDUCATED, HEALTH-CONSCIOUS CONSUMER

The consumer movement has expanded the public's medical knowledge. The information age has made it possible to find in-depth medical information fairly easily with the help of proliferating healthcare magazines, detailed and priority reporting in the news media, medical programs on radio and television, and widespread use of the Internet. The extensive news coverage of the medical problems of celebrities and political figures in recent years is a good illustration of the public's attention to medical information.

Many pharmaceutical companies have taken it upon themselves to expand promotional efforts into this vast area of medical information. They have developed consumer education initiatives, customer service hotlines, referral networks, and screening programs to detect diseases for which their products can be subsequently prescribed. Most companies now have Internet sites that include special areas for consumers offering detailed information, interactive capabilities, and coupons for rebates.

INDUSTRY GIANTS, GROWTH COMPANIES AND BLOCKBUSTER DRUGS

The pharmaceutical industry saw unprecedented consolidation through the 1990's, and it continued unabated in 2000-2002. In 1990, the world's top 10 players accounted for just 28 percent of the global market. Ten years later, that proportion is greater than 45 percent and still gaining. In 2001, the top ten companies represented 53 percent of the U.S. pharmaceutical industry. Even so, no individual player has a U.S. market share exceeding 10 percent. The U.S. market giants are listed according to 2001 sales in *figure 12.*

The largest merger was two sizeable British companies, Glaxo Wellcome and SmithKline Beecham, to form a $160 billion giant called GlaxoSmithKline. Pfizer completed its merger with Warner-Lambert (Parke-Davis), retained the Pfizer name, and is now worth $90 billion. Pharmacia & Upjohn completed their merger with Monsanto (Searle) and are now worth $23 billion under the name Pharmacia Corp. The latest mega-merger came in July of 2002 when Pfizer and Pharmacia agreed to merge in a transaction valued at $60 billion.

Mounting pressures from third-party reimbursement, looming patent expirations for major products, the need for rich product pipelines, and growing globalization of the industry are forcing leading companies to combine. The new drug giants are formidable forces on the global market. They also become more efficient by cutting operating costs, eliminating redundant marketing, manufacturing, and R&D efforts and can offer "one stop shopping" to managed care customers and other large buyers. They put the necessary resources toward important development and marketing of new billion-dollar drugs, known as blockbusters, to fuel ongoing growth. These medications are the lifeblood of the pharmaceutical industry giants. Current blockbuster products are listed by year 2001 sales in *figure 13.*

Many relatively smaller companies are showing incredible growth in 2000. Only the companies with greater than 20 percent annual growth are listed in *figure 14.*

FIGURE 12: TOP 10 INDUSTRY GIANTS BY GLOBAL PHARMA SALES IN 2001
Source: *IMS Health, Retail and Provider Perspective, 2002*

Organization	2001 Sales in Billions	% Market Share	Sales Force Size
Pfizer	17.6	10.0	8,200
GlaxoSmithKline	15.5	8.8	8,000
Merck	12.5	7.1	7,000
Johnson & Johnson	10.9	6.2	5,500
Bristol-Myers Squibb	10.5	6.0	5,200
AstraZeneca	10.0	5.7	6,000
Lilly	7.6	4.3	4,100
Wyeth	7.0	4.0	4,400
Novartis	6.8	3.9	5,900
Pharmacia	6.5	3.7	4,500

FIGURE 13:   TOP U.S. BLOCKBUSTER PRODUCTS BY U.S. SALES 2001
Source: *IMS Health*

Product	Company	Therapeutic Category	Diagnosis	2001 U.S. Sales in Billions
Lipitor	Pfizer	Cholesterol-reducing statins	Cholesterol	$5.2
Prilosec	AstraZeneca	Proton pump inhibitors	Ulcers	4.6
Zocor	Merck	Cholesterol-reducing statins	Cholesterol	3.7
Prevacid	Tap	Proton pump inhibitors	Ulcers	3.5
Celebrex	Pharmacia	COX-2 inhibitors	Arthritis, pain	2.6
Epogen	Amgen	Erythropoietins	Anemia	2.6
Procrit	Johnson & Johnson	Erythropoietins	Anemia	2.6
Zyprexa	Eli Lilly	Antipsychotics	Schizophrenia	2.5
Zoloft	Pfizer	SSRI	Depression	2.3
Paxil	GlaxoSmithKline	SSRI	Depression	2.1
TOTAL				**$31.7**

FIGURE 14: **Top Growth Companies by Percent Increase in Global Pharmaceutical Sales**

Source: ***Pharmaceutical Executive***

Company	2000 Yr. Sales in Billions	Percent Growth from '99	Sales Force Size (if available)
Forest Laboratories	0.87	60	1,500
Pharmacia	10.80	57	4,500
Alza (part of J & J)	0.48	48	
Teva	1.55	37	49
Purdue	1.35	34	
Elan	1.05	31	200
Chiron	0.63	31	
Novo Nordisk	2.48	27	1,000
Merck KGaA	2.33	26	240
Schering AG	2.51	24	780
Bayer	5.51	23	1,300
Genentech	1.28	23	500
Biogen	0.76	23	
Allergan	0.67	22	300

Chapter 2

The Sales Representative

In this chapter of Insight, you will learn about the actual job of the pharmaceutical representative. You will see that a challenging and rewarding career, and an excellent all around work life is yours for the taking. After a brief description of a typical workday, this chapter focuses on some of the normal challenges faced by the representative. Upon completion of this chapter, you will have a basic understanding of the entry-level position, and be able to answer the following questions:

- What is a Pharmaceutical Representative?
- What qualities are companies looking for in job candidates?
- What does the Representative need to know?
- How are they trained?
- What does a typical day look like?
- What does it take to be successful?
- What are some positive and negative aspects of the job?
- How are Representatives compensated, and what are the financial incentives?
- What are the career advancement opportunities?

In later chapters, you will learn how to dig deeper into the job, what the pharmaceutical market is, and uncover potential opportunities in your area. For now, take some time to review this chapter. It will give you the solid base of knowledge you will need to begin the networking process, described in Chapters 4 and 5.

WHAT IS A PHARMACEUTICAL REPRESENTATIVE?

For a perspective on this exciting position, begin with a look at some of the many titles used across the industry to designate the pharmaceutical sales representative. Behind these titles are individuals who possess a high degree of technical expertise, selling skills and professionalism.

Pharmaceutical Sales Representative	*Professional Representative*
Territory Manager	*Territory Sales Manager*
Hospital Sales Representative	*Institutional Sales Specialist*
Medical Representative	*Specialty Representative*
Medical Service Representative	*Hospital Specialty Representative*
Professional Sales Representative	*Senior Professional Representative*
Senior Sales Associate	*Account Manager, Account Executive*

For the pharmaceutical sales representative, the primary target audiences are physicians and pharmacists.

Obviously, you will be selling to highly trained and technically oriented professionals. Such an audience demands that you also have a high level of expertise. You must know your customers' business, your products, your competitors' products, and the diseases and health conditions for which your products are prescribed.

Does this mean you have to be a physician, a pharmacist, a nurse, or other health care professional in order to be successful? Absolutely not! The goal of the Pharmaceutical Representative is no different than that of any sales professional who provides a product or service. Pharmaceutical salespeople are professionals selling the goods and services of an organization. The key to success lies in thorough preparation to guide you in making effective sales calls and following up on your commitments. Success requires determination, attention to customer service, and hard work. It does not need a specialized degree in any one area. It is no different than selling in any other industry. That is why people from all sorts of backgrounds, educational levels, and previous sales experiences are successful in the pharmaceutical industry.

The 30th president of the United States, Calvin Coolidge, captured this concept in the following quotation:

> *"Nothing in the world can take the place of persistence. Talent will not; nothing is more common than unsuccessful [persons] with talent. Genius will not; unrewarded genius is almost a proverb. Education will not; the world is full of educated derelicts. Persistence and determination are alone supreme."*

Successful sales abilities in other product or service areas will transfer well to the pharmaceutical industry. Success is success!

WHAT QUALITIES ARE COMPANIES LOOKING FOR IN JOB CANDIDATES?

A job candidate needs to possess many skills. The essential qualities desired by a pharmaceutical company are generally the same as those of other sales organizations. Of course, you must demonstrate to prospective employers that you have the competencies that they are looking for in a new employee. You have to convince the first interviewer that you have the qualities that fits the profile his or her company has in mind. You can create the opportunity to do so by following the strategies outlined in this manual.

You will discover that these attributes can be demonstrated clearly in the way you approach and progress through the networking and interviewing process. Central to the strategy is the concept that the job search itself is an ideal opportunity to clearly demonstrate you own potential in a powerful way. You must sell yourself as the right candidate in order to get the job. This is the first opportunity that the interviewer has to assess your talents in sales. You are talking about your skills and at the same time demonstrating them. The employer is the buyer. It is similar to the selling situations you will face as an employee of your new company. Thus, be at your best in all your contacts with prospective employers from the very start.

Most companies have a definitive profile, and interviewers will tailor their questions to identify whether you fit this profile. Essentially, you want to plan and be prepared to illustrate, with examples, each of the qualities you possess. Familiarize yourself with the following attributes. These will bring you success in pharmaceutical sales.

- Results Oriented or Goal Oriented: Your activities are directed towards an identifiable, stated or written goal.
- Motivation: Show what makes you get up in the morning, and what excites you about the job and company you are pursuing.
- High Energy: The ability to produce large volumes of work and put in long hours if necessary.
- Flexibility: Able to perform well under changing conditions and demands.

- Communication: Simply put, communications are everything you do and say, and how you do it. As a sales representative, you are in the business of constantly communicating to your customers and your company. This includes listening, speaking, presentation skills, business writing skills, and telephone skills. Presenting yourself well from the start will go far in demonstrating that you have this talent.

- Determination: You have the intention to get what you want both personally and in business. You succeed in the face of adversity. You do not become discouraged, are not afraid to take risks, and you learn from your own mistakes.

- Drive: You have the zeal to achieve goals, and a sense of urgency to complete large and small tasks. You are not complacent or easily satisfied.

- Confidence: You are calm and attentive; you are not arrogant, but very sure of yourself in front of people. You have straight, relaxed posture, good eye contact, and voice projection. The best way to be confident is to be prepared!

- Reliability and Integrity: This is trustworthiness. It is being responsible for your promises and commitments to the customer. Follow-up is extremely important in pharmaceutical sales. For example, you may be asked a question for which you do not know the answer. How long will it take you to find out and communicate it to the customer? Pharmaceutical selling is an ongoing, consultative process. Your follow-up is what establishes your relationship as the customer comes to trust that you will always keep your commitments. If your customers trust you, they will also trust your company and your product. It is not only going the extra mile, but also going every mile.

- Listening Skills: It is a fact that salespersons talk too much instead of listening. Good listening is essential to strong relationships; it involves understanding and clarifying with questions what the customer is saying. With good listening skills, a customer feels heard and will be more receptive. These skills allow you to uncover customer needs so you can direct your product presentation to meet those needs.

- Creativity and Innovation: Create strategies, develop solutions to problems, and take advantage of opportunities. In pharmaceutical sales, for example, creative representatives think of unique, attention-getting ways of opening a sales presentation.

- Teamwork: As sales in the pharmaceutical industry changes to meet the challenges of the health care system, such as managed care, selling in a team approach is becoming more important. A sales team could include a sales representative, hospital specialty representative, managed care account manager, and district manager to achieve a common goal of increasing sales in a given managed care organization or physician group practice.

- Achievement: This can be shown by a history of success in other sales and career areas, in school, and community or extra-curricular activities.

Most employers commonly desire these attributes. They will provide you an excellent framework within which you are able to prepare for interviewing. However, an individual company or district manager may look for additional traits or possess certain "hot buttons." Hot buttons are specific attributes that a manager feels are especially critical, and they weigh most heavily in his or her selection of candidates. You can find out about these ahead of time through your contacts with a sales representative in that company (described in Chapter 5). During your networking, a good strategy is to ask for the desired requirements for the job as early as possible in the process. By uncovering these early on, you will be able to effectively match your skills and abilities to fit the needs of the company. You will perform this skill for product presentations once you are hired. During your preparation for the interview, determine specific examples from your past experience that you can present to illustrate each attribute you possess. This practice is critical to successfully interviewing.

WHAT DOES THE REPRESENTATIVE NEED TO KNOW?

Simply put, the Pharmaceutical Representative needs to be an expert in the medical specialty area in which his or her products will be used. That may seem daunting at first. How can you know as much as a physician or pharmacist who has all those years of training? There are several reasons you can accomplish this.

First, you will be dealing with a relatively small area of medicine compared to all of medicine. The physician or pharmacist has an extensive background involving hundreds of medications, many different disease states, and multitudes of treatment options. Your knowledge, on the other hand, will be highly specialized, focusing exclusively on a few medications you represent, only one or two diseases, and a limited number of treatment options. You will become an expert in your given areas.

Secondly, as a newly hired representative, you will embark upon an elaborate company training program. The pharmaceutical industry, as a rule, provides training and development that is unparalleled in any other industry. Most companies are proud of the extensive and demanding nature of their training programs. It is helpful in your research of each company to investigate its training program. You will learn when and how to approach this topic in later chapters.

Training is conducted in two broad areas. 1) Knowledge, which is the information you need about your products and your customers and 2) Skills, which are the learned behaviors and habits that you need in order to perform your job.

Examples of knowledge building can be found in the following:

- anatomy and physiology
- diseases for which your products are used, such as asthma, diabetes, cancer, and depression
- diagnosis and appropriate treatments
- your pharmaceutical products and competing products are referred to as product knowledge
- customer types and suggested selling approaches for each type
- the health care system managed care, retail pharmacy, etc.

Specific product knowledge on a medication that you promote is highly emphasized. For example, you will be required to know the following details about your products and their competition:

- mechanism of action (how it works in the body)
- indications of the medication (what it is used for)
- contraindications (when it may not be used)
- dosage regimens
- side effects
- warnings and precautions (under what circumstance is caution advised)
- current scientific medical studies
- costs of therapies

Examples of skill building are:

• call planning and preparation

- business planning and customer targeting, referred to as territory management
- listening and selling skills
- group presentation skills
- negotiation skills
- call reporting
- computer skills
- analytical skills, sales data interpretation
- strategic and creative processes
- teamwork, leadership, and managing your career
- setting up and managing a home office

Thirdly, many training sessions are company-specific. These include policies and procedures for working day to day within the corporate environment. Examples are reporting procedures for sales call activity, travel and entertainment expenses, and use of your company car.

Why do companies place so much emphasis and investment in training? The goal of each company is to represent itself in the best possible light. When you represent a company, you are the company to that customer. A physician must feel very confident in prescribing a pharmaceutical product. He is placing the health of his patient and his own reputation on the line with each treatment decision. Therefore, it is imperative that you project the utmost professionalism, confidence, and knowledge to that decision-maker.

It would be a liability for a pharmaceutical company if a representative were ill prepared and therefore misinformed its customer physicians. All statements made by a representative are considered "promotional claims" and must comply with FDA guidelines. Pharmaceutical companies must monitor this closely to ensure that their sales force is performing to this standard.

HOW IS THE REPRESENTATIVE TRAINED?

Training programs for all of the top pharmaceutical companies are similar. These programs usually begin with extensive at-home reading assignments, then two to six weeks of classroom sessions under qualified instructors including role playing sales calls and taking written examinations. Role-play situations are used to practice what you are learning. A trainer will play the role of a customer so the trainee can become familiar with questions and objections he or she will encounter during sales presentations. After this initial period, your training will move into the field. A trainer, manager, or experienced representative will work with you in your territory. You will also observe other representatives working in other territories. Your district manager or a trainer will work with you frequently at first, then perhaps every four to six weeks. Their role is to provide observation, insight, motivation, and coaching to your performance. You will need to be able to accept positive criticism well and have a desire to learn and grow. Many companies will use the training program as an ongoing evaluation of the candidate. You will discover challenges that are unlike those of any college program you have ever experienced. Be prepared to take it very seriously.

Training in the pharmaceutical industry never ends. You need to know about the new drugs that have been approved by the FDA, and the side effects of existing ones. This is an ongoing process. Medical science will continue to provide new advances and scientific breakthroughs for new products, new clinical research studies, recalled drugs, and uncovering new diseases. As in any sales industry, you will continually face the threat of new competitors and the advent of new market opportunities. Nowhere is this more the case than in today's ever-changing healthcare environment. This profession rewards the individual who builds his or her knowledge and skill levels.

WHAT DOES A TYPICAL DAY LOOK LIKE?

As with many other sales professions, Pharmaceutical Representatives work from their homes. There is no one to look over your shoulder every day. Your self-determination is the key to your success. You should emphasize your independent drive and self-motivation as you interview.

A typical day consists of presenting your products to physicians and pharmacists. You and your manager usually determine the specific number of calls you make. Your "call plan" is a list of targeted physicians in your geography. Armed with your call plan, sales data, corporate plan of action, sales support materials, product samples and literature, you will prepare for the day, week, or other period. Only then are you ready to venture out to make your calls on the customers.

Your company's "plan of action" (or similar term) helps you set your objectives for the day, including what products and promotional messages you will emphasize. The plan of action is based on the priorities of the company as determined by the sales management and marketing teams. To illustrate, imagine that your employer, XYZ Pharmaceuticals, Inc., has decided to promote their antibiotic for the next twelve weeks and is increasing the focus of their representatives' presentations to increase their market share in this product category. After this twelve-week period, selling focus may shift to promote a different product, perhaps a new line of oral contraceptives or anti-inflammatories. Promotional plans often are based on financial or sales periods, such as quarters or trimesters.

During your day, you will enter physicians' offices to make your presentations. You will be challenged to overcome the obstacles between you and this all-important customer. Obstacles include the constraints on the doctor's time, working with (or through) the office staff, and perhaps being bumped by one of your competitors! Your knowledge of the doctor's preferences and schedule, your rapport with the office staff, and other tricks-of-the-trade will help you meet this challenge.

Once you are in front of the physician, you may have a few seconds or several minutes to perform the skills and communicate the knowledge necessary to gain the doctor's confidence and commitment to prescribe your product. During this time, your preparation is the key to your success. You are a resource of information, providing unique services to the physician and ultimately the patient. Thus, you must understand the physicians' needs and attitudes in order to position your product to satisfy those requirements. Your final goal is to gain the physician's commitment to prescribe your product.

However, there are aspects of every industry that make it unique, such as product lines, customer audiences, decision-makers, the purchasing environment, sales cycles, call frequency, and others. The goal of selling pharmaceuticals is the same as for any product. However, this industry has some characteristics that are inherently different from other businesses. For example, the Pharmaceutical Representative does not sell directly to the end user of the product, or the patient. In other words, the "decision maker" does not actually buy or take the medication. In fact, the decision-maker (physician), the consumer (patient), and the payer (insurer) are all different individuals or organizations. The Pharmaceutical Representative presents his or her products to the prescribing physician, dispensing pharmacist, or other purchaser such as a hospital or managed care organization (MCO).

The decision-maker is generally the one who writes the prescription, or the physician. The pharmacist can also decide, in some situations, to dispense a product other than the one prescribed by the physician. This can happen in two ways. The first is generic substitution, whereby the pharmacist dispenses a generic form of the same medication that is prescribed. Secondly, the pharmacist may call the doctor and request permission to dispense a completely different medication, but one that has the same overall effect on the patient. This is a process called therapeutic substitution. Thus, both the pharmacist and the physician influence which medication the patient ultimately gets.

Further complicating the scenario is another decision-maker referred to as the "payer," or the "third party." Think of the patient as the first party, the health care provider (doctor, pharmacist, etc.) as the second party, and the person paying the bill as third party. Third parties are the insurance company, the employer, and the health plan or managed care organization (MCO), or the government in the case of Medicare, Tricare, Champus, and Medicaid. Examples of MCO's are health maintenance organizations (HMO), preferred provider organizations (PPO), and pharmaceutical benefit management companies (PBM). Managed care organizations do have impact in approving which medication the patient ultimately is given by limiting what specific drugs they will pay for or "reimburse." Enforcing a "formulary," which is a list of approved drugs that are "covered" or paid for by the MCO, does this. The formulary is sent out to all doctors and pharmacists to guide them as to which drugs should be prescribed and dispensed for patients enrolled in that MCO. Thus, third party payers are important customer audiences for pharmaceutical companies, particularly MCO's.

Because the prescribing physician and the dispensing pharmacist are the primary audience of the entry-level sales representative, Insight will limit the focus of discussion to include only office-based physicians and retail-based pharmacists. Other customers, such as MCO's, are the responsibility of experienced account managers and national account executives that have been promoted from sales representative and district manager positions.

Another characteristic of pharmaceutical sales is the unique selling process. First, the process of selling to a physician would not be characterized as a hard sell. There is no push to get the customer to "sign the bottom line" by using aggressive sales techniques and power negotiations. Rather, pharmaceutical selling is characterized as consultative. You are a consultant to the doctor, providing educational and informational data to support his or her decision to use your products. This is not to say that you do not gain a commitment from the doctor. You must close the sale aggressively if you are to change a doctor's behavior. You must ask the physician for a commitment to prescribe your products, and continually reinforce that commitment. However, you must earn the right to ask, and win the trust of the physician by providing product information, published literature, clinical studies, answers to any questions that come up, patient examples, medication samples, patient education materials, and whatever additional information the physician or pharmacist requires.

The physician is in search of the most medically appropriate product that will achieve optimal results for the varied needs they have. The biggest need, of course, is to provide benefits for the patient. A physician is basing his or her decision on years of extensive education and experience. They also possess unique characteristics, strong attitudes, or hot buttons, which drive their prescribing habits. For example, a given doctor may be more likely to use one medicine over another because it is new or perceived to be more scientifically advanced. This type of physician is an early adopter of new products. Another physician will do the opposite, preferring older and more proven therapies. This type of physician is a late adopter.

Other requirements affect the physician's decision to prescribe a particular medication. These are the professional and personal necessities of the individual physician. Many needs also arise from the physician's consideration regarding third party influences. Such third parties include the group practice in which the doctor is a member, a hospital system where the doctor is on staff, managed care organizations that provide a flow of patients to the doctor, governmental and other health plans, employers, and insurance companies. Your challenge is to uncover all the various needs and attitudes of a given doctor. You can then position the features and benefits of your products to best meet those needs and gain the commitment to prescribe. Physicians are creatures of habit like anyone else. They typically have a small group of medications they have become comfortable with and prescribe repeatedly. Changing their prescribing habits is your challenge.

It may take several sales calls on an individual physician before you successfully close the sale and the doctor prescribes your product. The selling cycle may be longer or shorter for some doctors, depending on the needs and attitudes previously described. A contrast is the retail sales environment, where a sale must be made on a single encounter with the customer. That is not always the case with a physician—it means that you may not ask for the business, or close the sale, on the very first call. Always ask the client for a commitment to try your product.

Another challenge awaiting you on a typical day is differentiating yourself from your competitors, as well as their products. As you now know, selling pharmaceuticals requires a technical and consultative approach. However, this fact does not obviate the benefits of relationship selling. People buy from people, as the saying goes, and physicians are no different. Developing good rapport with your customers is essential to gaining their time and attention. Physicians' offices have 75 to 100 individual sales representatives from different companies and industries calling on them. Sometimes the office staff will have five Pharmaceutical Representatives that call on them in a single day. They are busy and have limited time so it is your job to obtain the doctor's time and attention. Your excellent rapport, product knowledge, communication skills, and professional demeanor can set you apart from representatives of competing pharmaceutical companies.

Physicians differ in their overall attitude towards Pharmaceutical Representatives. These decisions span from complete refusal to speak with pharmaceutical salespeople to an open door policy. This range of mannerisms is one aspect of the job that offers a challenge to the representative. For example, you need to be innovative to create opportunities to get in front of the "hard-to-see" doctor.

Product samples and patient information may be a part of your total offering. If so, this provides the physician with an excellent service for his practice. Most physicians applaud the practice of free samples. These are used to start therapy or sometimes treat a particular patient with that medication. Often the doctor can evaluate the response to the drugs without having the patient incur the full cost of the prescription at the pharmacy. Sometimes physicians will provide a patient with two different medications (such as treatments for allergies), and have the patient try each one at home. The patient will decide which one works best. Physicians will also use samples to assist a patient who cannot afford the cost of the prescription. Product samples are an excellent service that can be offered to the physician who in turn can provide a better service to the patient.

A large part of the typical day is spent in planning, organizing, and reporting. You will manage your time by planning your calls for the day and routing yourself in the most efficient way, based on appointment times and customer locations. You will assemble all the necessary materials—sales information, visual aids, clinical studies, and product samples. It is important to stock and organize the supplies you need in your company vehicle. This will ensure that you have what you need and your day runs smoothly. Recording and reporting each call is also critical to your success. The method you employ will vary slightly by company. The advantages of recording call activity are that you can retrieve the information later, use it to evaluate your efforts and what you accomplished, remember what the customer commitment was, and importantly, what commitments you made and what you need to do next. Most companies now use laptop computers to enable you to instantly record your calls "in the field." Computers also offer you instant access to customer records and are an excellent tool for sales tracking.

WHAT DOES IT TAKE TO BE SUCCESSFUL?

Many personal characteristics and traits are essential to your success. These requirements were described in this chapter and will be revisited in later chapters—they are the qualities you will want to demonstrate during your sales interview process. The following keys to success are practical applications of your individual talents. This discussion will give examples of successful goals and strategies.

First, excellent product knowledge forms the basis of your sales presentations. Secondly, successful sales representatives consistently see the highest number of potential customer physicians within their territory, and deliver the correct message as set forth by the marketing department. They establish professional rapport with doctors and office staff. Perhaps you will not be friends with every physician you call on, but it is not essential to your professional relationship that you build your personal relationship. You need only have a few high-writing doctors on your client list to be successful. A good representative lives by the old 80-20 rule. That is, 80% of the prescriptions are written by 20% of the doctors.

What is good, professional rapport? It means learning the physician's needs, schedule, patient types, current prescribing habits, and hot buttons. Is he clinically or technically focused? Does he prefer a product because it is convenient, inexpensive, or new? Does he pay attention to all those managed care formularies or does he focus on what is best for the patient? Rapport also means trust. It is imperative that what you say is accurate and that you are dependable. It takes time to develop a sales relationship before an actual sale or commitment to prescribe can take place. There are no short cuts, and if you are to learn the intricacies of the industry, you will still need to give yourself two to three years in a given territory to really get up to speed and productivity. This concentrated time at the outset of your career will be invaluable as your progress, whether you remain in sales, pursue management, marketing, or even the office of the Chief Executive.

As you begin in your new territory, you will be assigned a selected audience of physicians, pharmacists, and hospitals. You will be on a schedule that puts you in front of the same customer every four, six, or eight weeks, depending on your company's direction. This schedule is your call cycle and determines your call frequency. The sale can sometimes require several contacts, which you will accomplish as you repeat your call cycle over time. Success is dependent on a consistent selling message, frequency of contacts, and professional relationships.

WHAT ARE SOME POSITIVE AND NEGATIVE ASPECTS OF THE JOB?

As with any career choice, there are positive and negative aspects of a career in pharmaceutical sales. In summarizing the most common job aspects we use the information that we acquired from numerous interviews and focus groups with pharmaceutical representatives.

The job requires autonomy in your daily activities. Some people enjoy this aspect and the freedom to be creative in their sales efforts. Others complain that such autonomy often leaves them feeling isolated from co-workers and without direction. Individuals who are not disciplined and self-motivated will find themselves struggling with distractions. Determination and a drive for success are essential attributes for this reason.

Job burnout can be a problem with Pharmaceutical Representatives just as it is with other demanding professions. One of your biggest challenges is to keep yourself motivated daily. The best way to do so is to set short-term, realistic goals. Look for new challenges and be creative. Have fun with it! Your district manager has experienced the same job stresses that you have, and is responsible for helping you stay motivated. He or she will be a good resource, but it will be mostly up to you.

There is a twelve- percent turnover-rate in the industry, which indicates that this job is not for everyone. Our research suggests that some Pharmaceutical Representatives become complacent in their positions over time and no longer experience the job satisfaction that was present in the beginning of their careers. The day-to-day work can become tedious, and it requires your own creativity and motivation to make it exciting. Having supportive management and a team spirit among your peers is also helpful. Calling on six to nine physicians per day, spending time in waiting rooms, idling in traffic, and going into pharmacies and hospitals is a hard day's work. Sometimes the heat of summer or freezing winter snowstorms challenges your resolve. Will physicians complain if you do not make the sales call? Hardly! Will your manager know if you ended your day too early every now and then? Probably not. Your determination and persistence will be the key to the success of your career.

Pharmaceuticalsales.com spoke with representatives who had 10 to 30 years on the job. On the positive side, many experienced veterans reported that job satisfaction increased over the years. The continual learning associated with new products and technologies offers unlimited challenge. The rapport and long-term relationships they have developed with their physicians and pharmacists are personally valuable and important. These long-term customers also appreciate the experienced representative and recognize good salespeople are a tremendous resource. Career sales representatives find satisfaction in the recognition they receive over the years. Multiple sales awards, generous raises, and commission payments come with hard work and experience. The number one reason given for long-term success is practicing a strong work ethic.

To summarize, individuals in this field are as unique as in any profession. You will discover whether this career is a good fit for you only through investigation and research—a process you have already started! Before you decide for or against this career choice, gain the broadest perspective, you can from individuals within the profession.

HOW ARE REPRESENTATIVES COMPENSATED AND WHAT ARE THE INCENTITIVES?

Compensation packages in the pharmaceutical industry vary from company to company. Typically, you will receive a combination of base salary plus a bonus or commission on sales achievement. Our research shows that the annual base salary for an entry-level representative may range from $35,000 to $45,000. Bonuses and commissions are generally paid out by quarter, trimester, or year based on sales performance. Industry norms show a wide variance in bonus structure, with annual earnings ranging from $5,000 to $25,000. Usually, the higher the base salary, the lower the bonus potential. Thus, the salary to bonus ratio is less important to look at than the sum of both.

To illustrate, consider a Pharmaceutical Representative who works for a company that pays a low base combined with a high bonus structure. Let us say this individual earns a base salary of $35,000, which is at the low end of the range, and is eligible to earn between $20,000 and $30,000 on bonuses and/or commissions. The total package is worth $50,000 to $60,000 per year. In another company, that same representative may earn a larger base salary, say $40,000, but only be eligible for a commission and bonus of $10,000 to $20,000. His total package is the same as in the first example. Again, this varies from company to company. The first-year Pharmaceutical Representative can usually expect a total package of $50,000 to $60,000. In addition, there is compensation for business and entertainment expenses, a company car or car allowance, excellent medical and dental plans, retirement and savings plans, and perhaps stock options. You can expect your base salary to increase yearly if you stay with the same corporation. Many companies have different pay levels associated with certain criteria of performance and length of service within the organization.

It is important for any representative to know how sales performance is measured. This is another topic for you to explore during your research into the industry and contacts with prospective employers. It is not advisable to inquire about the amount of compensation early in the interviewing process. However, you should inquire about the basics. For example, what methods of evaluation are used to measure job performance? What percentage of total compensation comes from base salary versus bonus and commission? This information will provide insight into the management style of the company. For example, if a company places emphasis on representatives' autonomy and creativity, they will reward this behavior by placing a larger percentage of total compensation into bonus or commission. Bonus and commission payments are at risk—they are yours to earn, or yours to lose!

Sales tracking and measurement in pharmaceutical sales is historically problematic. In recent years, it has become more of a science. In brief, there are vendors, or specialized companies, who make it their business to accumulate distribution and prescription data from the various points along the supply chain. Then they process it into usable data runs and sales reports, and make it available to pharmaceutical companies for purchase. Thus, your company can provide you with specific sales by market share, numbers of prescriptions written, and tablets sold by territory, zip code, and even by specific doctor.

An example is to follow a unit (or bottle) of prescription medication through the chain of distribution. First, it is shipped from the manufacturer to a wholesaler, then from the wholesaler to retail pharmacies. Each unit is tracked by its movement through various market outlets: chain and independent community pharmacies, mail order pharmacies, food store pharmacies, mass merchandise stores with pharmacies, hospitals, nursing homes, and HMO's. When that outlet is located in your territory, as determined by zip codes, you receive credit for the sale of that unit. There are some inconsistencies, such as when a patient has her prescription filled in a pharmacy in another Pharmaceutical Representative's territory. This seems to be consistent in all territories. In other words, you get credit for prescriptions that come into your territory at the same rate by which you lose them when they are filled elsewhere.

It is now possible to track sales by individual prescription, which is a much more accurate way to measure sales performance. Once a doctor writes a prescription and the patient has it filled, the representative responsible for calling on that particular physician is credited with the sale. In this system, it does not matter in which pharmacy or zip code the prescription is filled. It also gives you specific data on the prescribing habits of each one of your customers—an obvious benefit when it comes to evaluating and planning sales strategies for that doctor. This detailed level of data is very expensive for pharmaceutical companies to purchase. However, it is worth it because of its value in evaluating and targeting customers. Your time is also expensive for pharmaceutical companies, and you are more productive when you can target doctors that respond well to your selling efforts.

WHAT ARE THE CAREER ADVANCEMENT OPPORTUNITIES?

Advancement opportunities are available and achievable within the pharmaceutical industry. Directions in which to advance are many and challenging. Opportunities may be categorized into three different areas of career specialization, as follows:

- Career Field Sales

- Field Sales Management

- Corporate Support Functions

Advancements in these three categories are accessible to representatives from the entry-level sales position. Each area offers unique experiences, builds additional competencies, and opens more doors for increased responsibility and compensation.

First, field sales opportunities are positions available within different divisions or segments of the sales force. They offer increased responsibility, experience with new customer types, different products, and new career challenges and growth. As the health care system changes, organizations rather than individual practitioners may make decisions about treatment. Such organizations are physician groups, hospital systems, MCO's, and governmental agencies. This shift has created opportunities in the pharmaceutical industry as companies expand and adapt sales forces to service these newer segments of the marketplace. Examples include the following:

- Senior Sales Representative: A life-long career in sales can be rewarding and provide an excellent work-life. This promotion does not significantly change what you are doing, but acknowledges your experience and advancing skills. It is offered to reward those with long-term success as a pharma ceutical sales representative.

- Hospital Sales Representative: This promotion offers new customer types, professional settings, and selling situations. The environment is in teaching hospitals or univesities, including schools of med icine and colleges of pharmacy.

- National Accounts Representative: This position requires business shrewdness and knowledge of product distribution. The main accounts include wholesalers and retail pharmacy chains.

- Managed Care Representative: This is an advanced field position, targeting HMO's, PBM's, employ ers, and physician groups. It requires advanced knowledge of the payer environment and overall health system.

- Government Affairs Representative: Legislation and policy changes will influence the pharmaceutical industry. Pharmaceutical companies are involved at all levels of government. Customers include state Medicaid programs, regulatory and licensing boards, professional societies, and associations, state public health departments, and formulary committees. This position may involve lobbying and legislative activity.

The second category of career options is sales management. This position is usually referred to as District Manager (DM). The DM's responsibilities include hiring, coaching, and managing an entire district of seven to ten or more representatives. The DM reports to the Regional Director (RD), who has responsibility for five to ten DM's and their subordinates. At the top of the sales force is the Director of Sales, who may be a vice-president (VP), and reports to another VP, usually of sales and marketing, or directly to the CEO. This structure varies from company to company.

The third category includes opportunities in the corporate headquarters. Promotions exist for the ambitious sales representative in many different departments. Some of these positions are listed.

- Sales Trainer: Designs, develops and delivers all types of training.
- Marketing Manager, Product Manager: Develops sales strategies, forecasts, and promotional pro grams for the sales force to implement.
- Communications Manager: Develops sales and corporate communications material and programs in support of marketing and sales strategies.
- Professional Education Manager: Developing educational programs for physicians and pharmacists.
- Sales Administration or Sales Operations Manager: Logistical areas of the sales force, such as computer systems, call planning and reporting, supplies, and bonus compensation plans.

Each of these advancements will require a successful background as a Pharmaceutical Representative for a minimum of two to three years. Progression to Director-level appointments requires experience in the corporate headquarters or "home office." Regardless of your long-term aspirations, your short-term goal is to achieve an entry-level sales position. Once you are working in the industry, develop your knowledge and skills to the best of your ability. Use all the resources available to you through the training department, your manager, experienced representatives, and corporate headquarters contacts. Identify your strengths and weaknesses. Evaluate where you can make the best contribution to the company, how you can maximize your strengths, and what interests you the most. Communicate to your manager that you are interested in development and advancement. Evaluate your situation and develop your goals for the future.

Chapter 3

Best Foot Forward: Resumes, Cover Letters

RESUMES AND COVER LETTERS

Resumes should be meticulously crafted. Their main purpose is to prevent you from being quickly and immediately eliminated as a potential interview candidate. This is an important fact about resumes. They constitute that all-important "first impression" that can either land you an interview, or land you in the wastebasket. Twenty seconds is all the time the average manager takes to look over a resume and decide whether the applicant should be granted the opportunity to impress the management in person. You do not want your resume landing in the proverbial "on-file" Neverland from which few ever emerge.

Picture this scenario: XYZ Pharmaceuticals needs to fill several positions created as a result of sales force expansion. The Human Resources Department (HR) places an advertisement in the "job classifieds" section of the weekend newspaper. In addition, the local District Manager alerts her sales representatives to "keep an eye open" for potential candidates. The company also implements a contest to motivate recruitment efforts by employees and they employ a professional recruiter to make contacts and identify qualified candidates for interviews.

Combining multiple recruiting strategies produces hundreds and hundreds of resumes. It is typical for just a single classified advertisement in a large metropolitan newspaper to generate more than five hundred resumes.

So, what happens next to all the stacks of paper? Picture them being screened according to basic minimum criteria by an individual, perhaps HR personnel, specialist, or a secretary. After some are eliminated, the rest are reviewed again using higher then higher standards, as the stack grows smaller. Eventually, there are only twenty-five to fifty remaining. The resume stack has been sufficiently narrowed for the next step—the interviewing process.

Wait a minute! What did those remaining twenty-five to fifty applicants do that was so special? The answer may surprise you—it is what they did not do that made the difference. They did not make simple mistakes that resulted in rejection for the others. Certain mistakes make you unappealing to the prospective employer. In other words, employers are initially screening out, not in, their applicants from the stack of resumes.

Employers are looking for reasons to winnow out particular applicants based strictly on their resumes. This is an easier and less time consuming process than determining which applicants should be interviewed and can be done by an administrative person, such as a secretary or assistant. As the stack grows smaller, they reverse the process and begin to focus on specific criteria such as the career history, education, and recommendations from current employees.

So how do you get over the first hurdle? What were the basic criteria and higher standards being used in the XYZ Pharmaceuticals example? Pharmaceuticalsales.com will give you the answers to both of these questions in this chapter. Dedication to the pharmaceuticalsales.com approach in marketing yourself can and will put you in front of the interviewer. Pharmaceuticalsales.com provides basic guidelines for writing your resume and cover letter, with examples of both.

TWENTY SIMPLE RULES FOR RESUMES AND COVER LETTERS

After conducting focus groups and interviews with managers who have made numerous hiring decisions pharmaceuticalsales.com has derived the following guidelines. These twenty rules should keep you from being disqualified by your target company and being dropped from consideration before the interview.

Do not bother with mass mailings or blindly sending resumes to pharmaceutical companies. In the rapidly changing business environment of today, this approach is too passive. Unsolicited resumes rarely, if ever, get a response. Spend your time on building a network of contacts (see Chapter 5). Once you make direct contact with a potential employer and they agree to see you, then use your resume. Send it directly to the hiring manager and all your networking contacts, not to the corporate Human Resources Department.

1. Outward appearances count heavily. Regardless of how good your handwriting is, always and without exception, type everything. This includes the mailing address and your return address on the envelopes. Type directly on the envelope if possible. If not, type or print the information onto a white label, then affix it to the envelope. Many managers state they will not even open a handwritten envelope, and will discard immediately a hand written cover letter or resume. Use a large, full-size envelope. For an extra touch, the envelope should be big enough so you do not have to fold your resume. This will keep the neat and professional look to your resume and cover letter that you worked so hard to create.

2. Do not be tempted to use colored paper to differentiate your resume from the horde. No manager with whom we spoke ever gave favor or "extra points" for this. Instead, use 100% white cotton paper for your stock and envelope. No other color is more professional than white, period! Have your resume printed using a high quality laser printer. Print each resume separately and avoid using photocopies. This gives the final copy a neat, sharp contrast. Pharmaceuticalsales.com suggests that you have your resume and sample cover letters stored on a diskette. If you have your own computer, you can do this yourself. If not, a local copy center can type, format, print your entire resume, and store it on a diskette. In other words, the copy center can laser-print it off your own diskette, if you have it, or they will type and format it onto a diskette for you. Then it is a snap to print additional copies including any changes to your resume quickly and easily.

3. How should you send your resume? First, avoid the temptation to fax your resume. Even if you mail the original hard copy after faxing it, your faxed copy ends up being seen first, and probably most often. Always mail your resume. If timing is crucial, use an overnight mail service. You place value on your work by not faxing it and by sending it via overnight mail. It will get more notice and the person receiving it will respect it. Even if time is not an issue, pharmaceuticalsales.com recommends that you use overnight mail.

4. The cost of U.S. Postal Service Priority Mail is the lowest rate at around three dollars for delivery in two to three days. Express Mail from the U.S. Postal Service delivers overnight for an extra charge. In addition, the U.S. Postal Service can deliver mail to a post office (P.O.) box. Other overnight services do not have that capability. Finally, because it is mailed in a sturdy 8.5 X 11-inch cardboard envelope, it will be protected from damage and you can avoid folding it.

5. Personalize it! When you are sending a resume in response to a classified advertisement from the newspaper, you will find that the "want ads" often do not list the District Manager's, or Human Resource Representative's name. In this case, you have to rely on the pharmaceuticalsales.com strategies described in Chapters 4 and 5. Use these tactics to discover the appropriate names. Ideally, through your networking efforts, you will find contacts in the company who can inform you of opportunities before new openings are even advertised. If the person screening resumes sees their own name or a District Manager's name on your cover letter, they are more likely to pay attention to your resume. Many times, however, blind classified advertisements do not mention the company name. You should still respond with your resume and cover letter to these ads. You want every opportunity to interview

and gain offers. If you have been following the pharmaceuticalsales.com method of networking from before the advertisement was placed, you may already know which companies are hiring. You may be able to find out which company placed the advertisement anyway!

6. The format or style of your resume helps organize the content and makes it attractive and easy to read. Keep it brief. Resumes should be one side of one page in length. Try different formats to get the look you want. See the sample resume at the end of this chapter for a good format. Keep one-inch margins. Do not crowd the page with long sentences. Leave blank space between short items of information. Use a simple, easy-to-read font selection. Include your name, address, telephone number, and email at the very top of your resume. This will allow the hiring person to contact you even if your cover letter is discarded or otherwise separated from the resume.

7. Provide a clear objective. Only five percent of job applicants do this. Managers want people who want the job. If you take the time and effort to match them up, your career objective states that you want that specific job. Communicate one specific career objective, listed first after your name and address. This will tell the hiring person exactly what you want right now. It is the "hook" that gets the reader to continue reading the resume. State your objective clearly and simply. Do not be wordy, vague, or say anything about your long-term career goals. Avoid overused expressions about a "challenging opportunity" or a "progressive organization." Such verbiage is boring and communicates nothing. State your immediate job objective only. You can include more detail in your cover letter, if desired.

8. List your job history in descending chronological order, beginning with your present position. Next, list your education. There is one exception to this rule: If you have been in the workforce under one year, then list your education first followed by your brief job history.

9. If you have a grade point average over 3.0, then include that information. List awards and recognition you have received.

10. Do not list your salary history, current salary, or desired salary.

11. Do not list personal information such as age, date of birth, marital status, children, religious affiliations, and hobbies.

12. Leave out explanations or "reasons for leaving" previous positions.

13. List the time spent in each job, indicating the first and last calendar year in which you were employed. Do not leave any gaps in time.

14. Do not list personal or professional references on the resume. Type your references on a separate sheet of paper. List three personal references and three professional references.

15. Triple check for errors on your resume and cover letter. Make certain that you have used proper grammar, punctuation, and spelling. Typographical errors send the message that you are not serious about the job or you simply lack the skills to produce a proper letter and resume.

16. Make extra copies of your resume and put them in your interviewing file. Bring them with you to all your interviews. Offer your resume to the hiring person as you begin the meeting. He or she should have one already, but do not assume that they have it in front of them. Additionally, this proactive measure communicates that you are attentive and that you anticipate the needs of the interviewer and the customer.

17. Cover letters: The cover letter is essentially your way of thanking the employer for reviewing your resume and setting the stage for the interview. Always send a resume with a cover letter. Keep the body of your cover letter under 100 words in length. If you had the responsibility to read 500 resumes and cover letters, you would not want to read an autobiography, nor is the cover letter the place to write it. Your cover letter should be direct and to the point. State clearly that you want the opportunity being offered. Give a short history of who you are and what you do. Refer to the sample cover letter at the end of this chapter.

18. You have a lot of information to pack into 100 words or less. Get the readers attention by making it specific, or personalized, to them and their organization. Give contacts by name, such as, "Steve Brady suggested I contact you" for each company you reference. Refer to the company by name. Use a formal business format for your cover letter and sign it neatly and legibly. Your cover letter should match your resume in format, font, and paper stock. A paper clip affixing it to the resume is appropriate. Refer to the sample letter at the end of this chapter.

19. Finally, have a current resume prepared at all times throughout your career. Keeping an updated resume will come in handy as you apply for promotions within your company, or move to another company. Do not force yourself to write one at the last minute when an opportunity presents itself.

[SAMPLE RESUME: CANDIDATE WITH TWO YEARS SALES EXPERIENCE]

Janet Lynn Jones
1234 Summer Boulevard
Winter, PA 19123
Phone: (215) 555-3456
Fax: (215) 555-3450
jljones@aol.com

Career Objective:
Entry level position in Pharmaceutical Sales

Field Preceptorship:
Planned and performed three days of observation with experienced Pharmaceutical Representatives to gain knowledge and perspective into this career opportunity.

Experience:
1998 to present:

Account Specialist, Progressive Business Machines, Inc., Philadelphia, PA
Sales of office equipment and service contracts to 130 business accounts

* Increased sales over 50% ($79,000 in first year in territory)
* "Rookie of the Year Award" in 2001
* Awarded "Sales Executive of the Month" for August, September and November, 2001
* Launched two new product lines

Education:

* Bachelor of Arts in Marketing, Minor in Communications
* Southern Methodist University, Graduated 2000

Cumulative GPA 3.6

Science course completion in chemistry and biology

Earned four-year division one NCAA swimming scholarship

Residence Hall Council President

Staff, Campus Newspaper

[SAMPLE RESUME: CANDIDATE IS A STUDENT OR NEW COLLEGE GRADUATE]

Janet Lynn Jones

Home Address: School Address:
1234 Summer Boulevard   23 Flyers Avenue, Suite #1026
Winter, PA 19123   Walnut, OH 45874
(215) 555-3456   (419)-555-5947
jljones@aol.com

Career Objective:
    Entry level position in Pharmaceutical Sales

Education:
    UNIVERSITY OF DAYTON,   DAYTON, OHIO
    Bachelor of Science in Business Administration, May 2001
    Courses include Marketing, Chemistry, Statistics, and Computer Applications
    3.8 GPA in Major, 3.6 GPA Cumulative
    Listed: Who's Who in American Universities
    Dean's List: All semesters

    February 2001   XYZ PHARMACEUTICALS
    Pharmaceutical Preceptorship
    Worked with Pharmaceutical Sales Representatives for three days, gaining
    insight into the industry and the position. Increased knowledge about territory
    management, marketing and targeting while observing day to day sales activities.

Sales / Experience:
    2000-present
    EAST DAYTON COMPUTER   DAYTON, OHIO
    Salesperson, Retail computer store. Advised clients on hardware and software
    purchases. Performed cashier and quality control functions.
    Promoted to Assistant Manager.

    Summer   EARL'S DRUGSTORE   WINTER, PENNSYLVANIA
    1999   Pharmacy Technician. Cashier in large retail pharmacy. Checked
    stock in, took inventory, assisted with phone calls to patients and physicians.

    Part-time   UNIVERSITY OF DAYTON   DAYTON, OHIO
    1999-   Laboratory Assistant, Computer Lab. Assisted students during
                  laboratory hours. Cleaned and repaired computer equipment.

Skills:
    Microsoft Office, Lotus 1-2-3, WordPerfect, PageMaker

[SAMPLE COVER LETTER: REFERRED BY NETWORKING CONTACT]

August 24, 2002

Janet Lynn Jones
1234 Summer Boulevard
Winter, PA 23005

William Betts
District Sales Manager
XYZ Pharmaceutical Company
240 West Argonne Drive
King of Prussia, PA 19414

Dear Mr. Betts:

William Brady recently told me of an open sales territory in the Philadelphia district due to a promotion. He suggested I contact you.

I am excited about a career with XYZ Pharmaceuticals. From your current product portfolio and pipeline of new products, such as Aspirin XL, I know I will excel in such a challenging work environment. From my own research and from conversations with William, I know I can make significant contribution to your sales team.

I would like the opportunity to interview with you. I will contact you by telephone early next week to discuss it. My resume is enclosed for your review. Thank you for your time and consideration.

Sincerely,

Janet Lynn Jones

[SAMPLE COVER LETTER: NEW COLLEGE GRADUATE RESPONDING TO CLASSIFIED AD.]

August 24, 2002

Janet Lynn Jones
1234 Summer Boulevard
Winter, PA 23005

William Betts
District Sales Manager
XYZ Pharmaceutical Company
240 West Argonne Drive
King of Prussia, PA 19414

Dear Mr. Betts:

I am interested in the position of Pharmaceutical Representative (Philadelphia Inquirer, May 13). My resume is attached for your review.

I have focused my education towards a career in the pharmaceutical industry. During the last semester break, I spent three days with Pharmaceutical Representatives to learn more about the sales position.

From your current product portfolio and exciting new drugs in the pipeline, such as Aspirin XL, I know I will excel in such a challenging environment. I am confident that I would make a successful addition to your sales team.

I want the opportunity to prove myself in your interviewing process and as a successful sales representative for XYZ Pharmaceutical Company. I look forward to your reply.

Sincerely,

Janet Lynn Jones

Chapter 4

Vital Research

Pharmaceuticalsales.com encourages you to market yourself to others who work in the industry. This process is known as "networking," which simply means getting to know people and letting them get to know you. All it entails is presenting your professional skills and abilities effectively to a specific audience for a business purpose.

What do networking and research have to do with each other? Networking is the "people" preparation that goes hand in hand with the "paper" preparation that we call networking. There is a cardinal rule at the core of the system one that you have heard many times, especially if you have been a Scout. That rule is BE PREPARED. You will find all the tools you need for success in this chapter and the next two. Chapter 5 launches you into people preparation, but let us start here with the paper preparation.

Upon completing this chapter, you will:

- Understand helpful techniques for research and finding sources of information.
- Develop a system to keep any vital information readily accessible, including the use of pharmaceuticalsales.com profiles provided in the appendix.
- Be able to demonstrate to a potential employer that you prepare yourself and show them the benefits to the company when they hire you.

WHY DO YOU NEED TO PREPARE YOURSELF?

The first major pay-off for being adequately prepared is that you are relaxed and confident. Your performance in networking and interviewing situations improves considerably when you are poised and thinking clearly on your feet. The candidate who is unprepared will never be at ease in the situation and will be afraid of what might come next in the interview. This distraction can cause you to stumble over easy questions and results poor listening skills and ineffective communication.

Secondly, good district managers are looking for adequate preparation. They know that the individual who prepares well for an interview is demonstrating a key aspect found in the successful sales professional. The manager will correctly assume that, because you are well prepared for your interview, you are the kind of person who will be motivated to prepare well for a sales presentation. The reverse is also true. In other words, why should a manager hire a person who does not take the time and effort to excel in an interview? Will something happen to motivate that person when he or she is hired? No! The manager wants to see you demonstrating now those things you say will do for the company later. Thus, the under-prepared candidate has already missed the opportunity to show that he or she is capable of self-directed research and education, a habit that directly relates to success in pharmaceutical sales. Show your motivation.

Next, a manager will be more likely to hire the candidate who knows what is expected in their career rather than someone who is blindly seeking any type of employment. By having, an understanding of the pharmaceutical industry and the specific company with whom you are interviewing you set yourself apart. You can show excitement for specific products or a recent increase in sales, for example. You can emphasize aspects of your background and personal attributes that relate to the company or product. You can say with confidence that you want to work for this company because you have done the research and know the business and professional commitments of the organization. You will shine when asked the inevitable question, "Why do you want to work for XYZ Pharmaceuticals, Inc.?"

What Does It Mean To Be Adequately Prepared?

Being prepared means that you know what to expect, are ready, and will not only participate in but also control your interview. You should be prepared with your answers to typical questions. Also, be ready to ask smart ones of your own. You should be able to demonstrate a basic understanding of a sales representative's job in the pharmaceutical industry, and of the specific company with which you are interviewing. These aspects are presented in following chapters of *Insight*. The central point of this chapter though, is to teach you how to conduct industry research, which is an integral part of the preparation you will need for successful networking and interviewing.

Where do you get the information? Industry information is accessible from these general areas:

- consumer media sources
- company published information
- business publications
- industry publications
- internet sites
- consumer media sources

The most readily available source is the everyday consumer media. The news media frequently and fervently reports on health issues, and consumers are listening. Public awareness is high due to health issues which attracts attention and raises viewer ratings. These easily accessible sources of information include the following:

- local newspapers
- national newspapers, such as *The Wall Street Journal* and *USA Today*
- news magazines, such as *Time* and *Newsweek*
- business periodicals, such as *Forbes, Fortune,* and *Crain's*
- television news magazine broadcasts, such as Dateline NBC and 20/20

You can start building your own awareness by reading these reports as part of your normal routine. Peruse the daily newspaper for health and medical related stories. Look for any headlines on healthcare, managed care, insurance companies, medical breakthroughs, new prescription drugs, and pharmaceutical manufacturers. Read each article with a questioning eye. What are the issues? What is the main message? Who wrote this and what is the author's perspective? You will not need to buy many subscriptions if you make a habit of stopping by the public library to browse and read. You can also obtain copies of pertinent articles for later reference.

Consumer media sources are also good for information on specific medications. Look for advertisements of prescription drugs in magazines and television commercials. In the ad, the manufacturer is communicating the features and benefits of their product. This will give you insight into how they are positioning the product in the marketplace. Who is the manufacturer? What features are being publicized and what are the benefits to the patient? Some print advertisements include an abbreviated version of the package insert, which is also called "drug labeling." This is in the fine print section, and it lists indications (under what circumstances the drug is to be used), side effects, dosages, patient instructions, and a brief explanation of how the drug works. Television and radio ads also give information about important side effects.

TIP: *For complete drug labeling information, look in the public library for* The Physician's Desk Reference (PDR). *This book is published annually by Medical Economics, and contains the complete drug labeling for every currently marketed prescription pharmaceutical product and many of the over-the-counter drugs.*

TIP: *Excellent baseline information is available through multiple media sources. Educating yourself on healthcare and the pharmaceutical industry is an excellent way to develop life-long learning habits. However, for more specific and in-depth information, locate a medical library where you can have access to the medical journals and references. The best resources are medical school libraries, large "teaching" hospitals, and other university settings.*

TIP: *Software programs such as Medical Drug Reference provide full descriptions of drugs, and can be used to check the interaction of different medications. Imagine the professional relationship that can be forged by a Rep who can respond to a doctor's question about specific patient issues within a very short period of time.*

Besides accessing general healthcare and pharmaceutical industry information, what can you do to get the business and marketing information you want before interviewing? Where can you find the details about a specific company's financial performance, sales force size, product line, and products currently in research or awaiting Food and Drug Administration (FDA) approval?

There are two main sources for detailed company-specific information:

- company published sources
- sales representatives working for that company

Chapter 5, "Networking," will discuss interacting with Sales Representatives. Until you have built, your contact network read the company-published sources. Examples of these are annual reports, 10K filings, current marketing initiatives, and marketing material. Annual reports are available in most cases by calling, writing, faxing, or e-mailing the corporate headquarters, and some companies have web sites with an option that allows you to order annual reports on-line. Ask for reports from the last two or three years. You should receive them in a few days.

After you receive the annual report, study it carefully. Write down any questions you may have about the organization. Read the annual reports chronologically. Is the company on track with its own agenda? Are forecasters' goals being met? Are new products making it to the marketplace as promised in previous years' reports? What is the corporate direction?

Next, directories such as Standard & Poor's and Dunn & Bradstreet are good sources of recent information. All public companies must file a "10K Report" every quarter with the Securities and Exchange Commission (SEC). These are abbreviated annual reports, and they are available to you at local libraries that offer a business index.

TIP: *A "trick of the trade" for keeping up with companies over the long term is to purchase a single share of stock. You will receive annual reports automatically every year, and will find it more interesting to track drug company stocks. What a surprise it would be for a manager to hear during the interview that you are a stockholder. You will surely be remembered for it.*

Your research should also include a review of the business newspapers and periodicals. These include *The Wall Street Journal, Crain's Business, Business Weekly, Forbes,* and *Fortune.* You can use the business index to search for all published articles on a specific company by name. You can then request back issues from the reference desk and read the articles. The most common type of storage is on microfilm, which makes it easy for you to browse nearly all of the publications. Call around to different libraries until you find one with a business index and access to previously published articles.

Your company-specific research should also include a thorough review of the company's Internet web site. These sites are an excellent source for company overviews, product summaries, drug labeling, stock trends, employment opportunities, and even employee benefits. Internet addresses are increasingly available on most company-published materials and advertisements. Of course, searches using the company name or product name will also result in finding the site you want. Pharmaceuticalsales.com has listed many company web site addresses in the "Company Profiles" section of *Insight* and provided additional on-line resources at the end of this chapter.

Your research may also include trade journals of the pharmaceutical industry. These publications often discuss prevailing and emerging business trends, profile organizations, review products, and highlight key individuals. Some examples are *Pharmaceutical Executive, Medical Advertising,* and *F-D-C Reports*. Thousands of libraries subscribe to electronic information-retrieval services, such as Nexis, that will speed your research. A listing of the more helpful references is available in the "pharmaceuticalsales.com Suggested Resources" at the end of this chapter.

HOW DO YOU KEEP AND READILY ACCESS VITAL RESEARCH INFORMATION?

You may be collecting articles and doing research over the course of a job search that could last weeks, months, or longer. It may be quite a while before you need to access that information for networking and interviewing. How will you keep track of everything you want to remember or save for future reference?

You need to have a storage method for important research and networking information that is easy to use. We suggest that you create a file on each company for which you have collected information or with whom you have made contact. Save general industry information that does not pertain to any single company in a separate file. As you find articles on companies of interest clip or photocopy them. Take notes during your research and add these to the appropriate file. You can also add product advertisements, computer printouts of web site information, and package inserts that you can collect from pharmacies. All of this will come in handy in preparing for, and in conducting, your interview.

Additionally, you need to document your networking contacts and track your telephone calls, meetings, and correspondence. Save your notes on all calls and interactions with sales representatives and managers, your meetings, and your interviews. Maintain your current resume as well as the original one that you sent to the company. Also, keep copies of your resumes, cover letters, thank you notes, and follow-up letters in another readily accessible file.

COMPANY PROFILES

Pharmaceuticalsales.com has provided a head start for you by creating company profiles of the top 35 pharmaceutical organizations. You can find these Company Profiles in the Appendix. The Profiles include organization overviews, telephone numbers, addresses, web sites, and current product portfolios.

In the final section of this book we have included several worksheets for recording your own notes and research as you prepare for interviews that lead to an exciting career. These worksheets can be removed from the book and kept in your file on each company. You may make photocopies for additional blank worksheets. Using the Company Profiles is also discussed in Chapter 5.

YOUR NEXT MOVE -- NETWORKING

Networking is one of the most important sources of vital company information, and should be an integral part of your research. Your resources are the many current representatives of pharmaceutical companies. Interacting with these people is the way to find out what is important to their respective organizations right now. Furthermore, it allows you to discover what is happening in your region of the country and in specific districts and sales territories. You can uncover success stories, identify essential challenges facing the company, and learn how you can contribute to the organization. Discovering this information first hand from sales representatives will round out your "paper" research. This is a critical part of your interview preparation. The pharmaceuticalsales.com method is described in depth in Chapter 5.

The advantage of performing all this research is realized only if you successfully demonstrate your expertise in the interview. There are several approaches and you may want to use all of them. Now that you have done the preparatory work, how can you best leverage your efforts?

- How do you demonstrate to a potential employer that you are prepared?
- How are you differentiated from other candidates?
- What is the benefit of hiring you?

As mentioned above, an important benefit to you is the confidence that comes from knowing you are ready. Your confidence will show in your voice, eye contact, and posture. Stand and sit straight, look the interviewer in the eyes, and project your voice loudly by breathing deeply from the diaphragm.

A second benefit, of course, is your ability to discuss specific company information. Make a point of presenting it. Take advantage of the natural flow of the dialogue to interject what you know. Show that you have done your research. You will appear energetic and attentive to detail. It will show you went the extra mile to learn something about the company. Here is an example:

> Interviewer: "The company will launch a new wide spectrum antibiotic this fall."
> Candidate: "Yes, I read about the unique once-a-day dosage of your new entry. It appears to offer benefits to patients and physicians treating pneumonia."

Also, be sure to include names of company individuals you have met with or talked with on the telephone. Here is an example:

> Candidate: "When I met with Steve Brady, I learned that the sales force is currently undergoing product training for your new ulcer medication. I understand there are several other new products under development as well."

As you are presenting your professional strengths, a brief description of your research and networking method makes a great example of your self-motivation, determination, and other attributes. Bring along your company file and lay it on the table as you talk. If the interviewer shows interest in this, which he surely will, go into more detail and show off what you have.

TIP: *Begin your interview by making the point that you are prepared. State in your opening remarks, "I have researched the XYZ Pharmaceutical Company and the sales representative position. I am an excellent fit for your company." This opening statement will often get a curious response such as, "OK, tell me what you know about the company." The ball is in your court and you are doing just what you prepared to do. Your effort is paying off. You have taken control of the interview.*

Next, you can demonstrate your preparation by providing specific company information. You can also do this by asking intelligent questions. Use specific company information as a lead-in to your questions to the interviewer. Add a prepatory statement that first gives information about the company. For example:

> Candidate: [give information] "I understand that XYZ Pharmaceuticals is focusing on

diabetes and high blood pressure medications. [ask question] On what diseases or therapies does the company want to focus in the future?"

TIP: *Clip and save prescription drug advertisements from consumer magazines and medical journals. Publications such as the Journal of the American Medical Association or the New England Journal of Medicine, are good sources for this. Preferably, find an advertisement for a medica tion manufactured by the company with which you are interviewing. Bring it to the interview and make a sales presentation to the interviewer on the advertised product. Use the advertise ment pages as your sales "visual aid" and make a commanding product presentation as if you were talking with a doctor. Be sure to ask for the commitment from "the customer" to prescribe your "product."*

A FINAL WORD ON RESEARCH

Surprisingly, less than one-third of interviewing candidates will perform the industry and company-specific research. You will differentiate yourself by doing so. Of those willing to learn about the industry and organization before the interview, only 1% of these candidates will perform the networking type of research. These people are the ones who will achieve their desired results.

- Research will take you into networking.
- This is where you will gain vital knowledge about the company.
- Professional pharmaceutical sales representatives and other contacts know the routines of the business.
- Through these resources, you will discover up-to-date information about the organizations.
- Know your sales region of the country.
- Prepare for job relocation.
- Identify key challenges facing the company.
- Discover ways you can contribute to the organization.

This will help you secure yourself a position among the proven 1% who virtually guarantee their success. Challenge yourself to execute the research and begin today!

SUGGESTED RESOURCES

This list contains suggestions for resources from each of the following categories:

- Business Periodicals
- Pharmaceutical Industry Periodicals
- Medical Journals
- Internet Resources

Business Resources

Dunn and Bradstreet's *Million-Dollar Directory:* Lists 160,000 companies that are both publicly and privately held; updated annually.

Standard & Poor's *Register of Corporations:* Lists 45,000 companies with insight to thousands of company executives.

Corporate Technology Directory (Corporate Technology Information Services): Focuses on the products of 35,000 companies including pharmaceuticals.

Personnel Executives Contactbook: Lists key personnel and other contacts of 30,000 publicly and privately held companies and government agencies.

Directory of Corporate Affiliations (National Register): Lists information on a company's corporate divisions and subsidiaries.

Industry Resources

pharmaceuticalsales.com Profiles: *Insight*, Appendix A, which lists vital information on 35 pharmaceutical organizations including company overviews, telephone numbers, addresses, web sites, and current product portfolios.

Pharmaceutical Executive: A pharmaceutical business and marketing publication that is published monthly. These are available at medical libraries and on-line at pharmexec.com

Med Ad News: A pharmaceutical business and marketing publication published 12 times a year. It may be available at some medical libraries. Engel Publishing Partners 609-530-0044.

F-D-C Reports ("Pink Sheets"): Current news information about the FDA and pharmaceutical R&D. These may be available at medical libraries.

Pharmaceutical Representative: The only newsmagazine solely for pharmaceutical sales representatives. Available from McKnight Medical Communications (rate $35.00 for 12 monthly issues). Telephone: 847-647-0259. They have a directory of regional and local Pharmaceutical Representative associations, which is also available on-line: http://www.medec.com/pr/

The Certified Medical Representatives Institute (CMR): CMR offers continuing education and certification for pharmaceutical sales representatives. You may want to consider certification once you begin your career in the industry.

Medical Journals

The following are common and respected medical journals that can be found in medical libraries and many public libraries:
* *New England Journal of Medicine*
* *Journal of the American Medical Association (JAMA)*
* *Medical Economics*
* *American Journal of Medicine*
* *American Druggist*

INTERNET RESOURCES

Company and Industry Research

These sites are good for background information on specific companies or general industry research.
* www.pharmaceuticalsales.com
    Our site offers numerous links to compliment your research. Many are listed below.
* http://www.coreynahman.com
    This is the premier site for both prospective and experienced sales representatives. It is a one-stop shop for industry news, company information, drug information, career information, resume review, industry links, and more.
* www.go2pharmsales.com
    An excellent source for opportunities in pharmaceutical sales

- www.quintiles.com

    These very specific industry trends are used by the pharmaceutical industry. Requires login.
- www.pibg.org

    Pharmaceutical industry benchmarking group provides interesting pharmaceutical case studies.
- http://www.imshealth.com

    Industry insights, trendlines, solutions spotlight; requires login for advanced information.

Big picture industry news and trends

- www.pharmexec.com

    Web site of Pharmaceutical Executive magazine
- www pharmweb.net

    Source for industry news and links.
- www.pharminfo.com

    Comprehensive information on prescription drugs. Experts answer questions online.
- www.Smartbrief.com

    Daily updates on news in the pharmaceutical industry.
- http://www.npcnow.org

    Pharmaceutical Council (NPC) is supported by more than 20 of the nation's major research-based pharmaceutical companies. NPC sponsors a variety of research and education projects.
- www.phrma.org

    Pharmaceutical Research and Manufacturers of America — Member List and links
- www.pharmrep.com

    Pharmaceutical Representative Online: The Only Newsmagazine Designed Solely for the Pharmaceutical Representative.

Online pharmacies are worth a look for general knowledge

- www.drugstore.com
- www.pharmabrowser.com

    Pharma Browser. Information on all companies. Requires a modest fee.
- www.pharmalive.com

    Industry/company news and links
- www.eyeforpharma.com

    Industry news, events, channels, free e-mail newsletter.
- http://www.fcg.com

    FCN Consulting group. This provides industry news, public policy news links.
- www.pharma-lexicon.com

    Searchable database will contain the address and contact details of every Pharmaceutical Company in the world. In addition, this site has a search feature to find the meaning of any abbreviation.
- http://www.wsrn.com

    Search Wall Street Journal's company research site

- www.edgar-online.com/
    Company business information, such as SEC filings
- www.fuld.com
    Links to industry specific pharmaceutical and biotechnology resources; some examples are: Centers for Disease Control, Dictionary of Pharmaceutical Medicine, drug information.
- www.biofind.com
    Biotech job and company information. It has an interesting section devoted to rumors in the industry.

Career Sites and Recruiters ("headhunters")

Networking, as described in Chapter 5, should always be your primary strategy. When visiting a searchfirm site, submit your resume. Follow that submission within a few days with a telephone call and speak to a recruiter at the firm. Then submit a thank you note and hard copy of your resume by mail.

Use these web sites to post resumes, and learn about openings. On some sites you can read and post messages about specific companies from employees and job seekers. For example, vault.com has a "Pharmaceuticals Message Board" and many posting areas for specific pharmaceutical companies.

Pharmaceuticalsales.com lists the following searchfirms to compliment your search.

- www.vault.com
- www.sixfigurejobs.com
- www.horanmedsearch.com
- www.bioview.com
- www.bowdoingroup.com
- www.hotjobs.com
- www.monster.com
- www.medsearchusa.com/
- www.amrjobs.com
- http://msajobs.com/
- www.medzilla.com

Education

Interested in an education in pharmaceutical marketing? There are several programs available. Check this site for more information.

- Pharmaceutical Marketing MBA at St. Joseph's University
- http://www.sju.edu/PHARMACEUTICAL_MARKETING

Chapter 5

Networking News

This chapter describes a unique way for self-marketing within the pharmaceutical industry. This method is the key to successful employment. Read this chapter well and put the strategy into practice.

You have probably heard the old adage, "It's not what you know, it's who you know." This expression refers to breaking into business opportunities and moving up the corporate ladder. Now, forget all about that old adage and relearn it the following way: "It's who you learn to know and who gets to know you." Moreover, "what you know" is just as important. Does this make sense? Maybe not now, but it will after you read through and apply the networking principles outlined for you here.

This chapter will provide a sure-fire way for you to market yourself in the targeted environment. The "pharmaceuticalsales.com way" will be your primary strategy, and will complement your efforts in other, more common, methods of job-hunting. You will still be checking the newspapers and responding to want ads, but you will also want to contact local and national executive search firms. Remember, everyone else is also checking want ads and talking to recruiters. What you will do in addition to what everyone else is doing is what will set you apart.

What you need to do is simple, and it works. It has been proven effective by many individuals currently in the industry and by others who have used it themselves and coached candidates.

The overall goal is:

• Become familiar with representatives working in the pharmaceutical market in your location, and make them familiar with you.

By following the strategy described in this chapter, you will accrue the following advantages:

• Obtain inside information about an opening in your area before it is advertised.
• Be known (and well thought of) by the employer before an opening even exists.
• Demonstrate your initiative and creativity to potential employers.
• Establish important relationships with individuals in the pharmaceutical industry.
• Possess detailed knowledge about the pharmaceutical industry, specific companies, and the job for which you are interviewing.
• Demonstrate your detailed knowledge of the pharmaceutical industry.
• Know the key individuals who do the hiring within your geographical area.
• Obtain an interview before a position is available to the general candidate market.

Okay, now you want to begin. What do you do next? First, create your own database of current pharmaceutical industry professionals working in your desired geographic area. You can employ various means to accomplish this. Here are some suggestions:

Visit a physician's office. Typically, doctors' offices have from 25 to 75 sales representatives from various industries calling on them—mostly from the pharmaceutical industry. Explain your desire to enter the pharmaceutical sales profession and ask if they will photocopy the business cards of all the Pharmaceutical Representatives who call on their office. Often, these business cards are filed together and can be easily accessed by an office secretary or nurse. You may want to start with your own doctor, or if you do not know one, the doctor of a family member. Do not be afraid to walk into a physician's office cold. Be sure to tell them what you are doing and ask for their assistance. You may experience rejection of course, but that is just part of being a salesperson. Keep trying different offices until you get what you want. Dress as if you were going to an interview and conduct yourself professionally.

TIP: *Speak directly to the physician about recommending a specific Sales Representative for you to contact. Ask for a name that stands out as someone they like and consider an excellent Rep. Also, speak with the office nurse and other staff while you are collecting your business cards.*

When you contact each Pharmaceutical Representative make it a point to inform them that the doctor specifically mentioned them as being exceptional or outstanding in their field. If possible, state exactly what the doctor or any member of the staff has said. This is a positive way to break the ice when you introduce yourself.

Apply these same successful strategies when you visit a hospital or retail pharmacy. Always ask for copies of their representatives' business cards. If you explain what you want to accomplish, most pharmacists are willing to help you.

TIP: *Independent pharmacists, rather than large chain pharmacies, may be more likely to keep a file of business cards. They may be familiar with local representatives and be willing to share information. Pharmacies are not always the best source because not every company in the area will call on pharmacies.*

Another way to develop contacts is to call your state or local pharmacy association. Explain your desire to enter the pharmaceutical sales profession and ask if they will recommend a few contacts so that you can learn more about the industry.

Once you have collected your business cards, add them to the network file you have been building during your search. Pharmaceuticalsales.com worksheets are provided at the end of the book. Now you are ready to start making telephone contacts. We have some suggestions to help you ask questions during your initial contact that will produce your desired result. The goal of this phase is to gain job information, get to know pharmaceutical industry personnel, and make it known that you are a job candidate. Please read Insight entirely before you begin this networking phase.

Once you have the business cards of various representatives, make a few calls per day, perhaps three to five. Simply, choose a corporation from Profiles (maybe you have even seen a want ad for an opening there) and dial the number. Explain briefly who you are and the purpose of your call—that you are interested in pharmaceutical sales as a profession, and you would like to meet to discuss it. Always ask the person if it is a convenient time for them, or if another time would be better. Let them know that you are willing to fit their schedule. The evening is best because representatives are out making sales calls during the day. Do not be shy!

Here is an example of how you might begin the telephone conversation:
> *"Hello, Ms. Young, my name is Janet Jones and I am interested in a career in pharmaceutical sales. Is this a good time to call you? I was given your card by Dr. Wellborn who suggested you would be a valuable resource because of your professionalism, and that you might be willing to help me. I would like to talk about your profession. When is the best time for you? I will work my schedule around yours."*

Remember to conduct yourself professionally. As the saying goes, "You never get a second chance to make a first impression." Put yourself in your "interview mode" because this helps you prepare to be the best candidate for the job. Treat all contacts in your networking process as potential interviewers and as potential co-workers! Be upbeat, positive, and professional. If your contact will meet with you, then you have achieved your first goal. A personal meeting is more memorable, gives you greater opportunity to sell yourself, establishes rapport, and builds relationships.

Some contacts may decide they would rather not meet with you, but would be willing to give you time on the telephone. Be prepared for this situation. Ask when would be a good time to call back, then during that follow-up call proceed with your discussion and questions as you would in a face-to-face meeting.

Many representatives will gladly share their time and expertise while there are others who will not. Respect their wishes and remain professional as you thank them for their time. Remember that rejection is common in sales at all levels. Never forget that you are a salesperson who is marketing yourself in this situation. At times, you will be turned down. Even a refusal adds to your knowledge base, which helps your career potential. Every sales person knows that there is a certain percentage of failure in his or her sales calls. Your persistence will pay off.

Another situation you should prepare for is the answering machine. Voice mail is more common than voice-to-voice contact. You can use that fact to your advantage by being prepared ahead of time with a concise message. State your name, purpose of the call, and inform them that you will call again later. Here is an example of a voice mail message you might leave for a networking contact:

> *"Hello, Ms Young, my name is Janet Jones. I am interested in a career in pharmaceutical sales. Dr. Wellborn suggested that you would be best to provide some insight into pharmaceutical sales, and gave me your card. The purpose of my call is to discuss this with you. I will call again to speak directly with you. Thank you for your time."*

Note that you do not ask the contact to call you back. Take the initiative to make the connection yourself. You must attempt to reach the person, calling at various times of the day and evening, and leaving a concise message each time. Use your information sheets in Profiles to make notes on your calls. After you have tried to reach them two or three times (and left a brief message each time so they know you tried), it is appropriate to leave your number and ask for a return call. Here is an example of such a message:

> *"Hello, Ms. Young. This is Janet Jones calling. I would like to speak with you about the pharmaceutical industry, and have been unable to reach you after several tries. Would you please return my call at a time most convenient for you? My telephone number is 555-5555. If you get my answering machine, please let me know the best time for me to call you back, and I will do so. Thank you."*

Keep your messages brief and to the point. This helps you make a good impression. Your new network contact will sense that you are not likely to take up much time. If your contact wants to offer their time, he or she can certainly do so and will gladly call you back.

Use the same brevity and professionalism in recording your own outgoing message for your incoming calls. Avoid gimmicks and background noise. Identify yourself by name, telephone number, and request that the callers leave a time for you to return their call. Here is an example of an outgoing message:

> *"Hello, this is Janet Jones, at 555-5555. I am currently away from my telephone. Please leave your name and number and when it is a good time for me to return your call and I will do so. Thank you."*

Because you are asking people to call you back, be prepared for their call. The value of using Profiles is that you can find needed information quickly when they do. You should have made notes of your previous contacts in Profiles. It is perfectly fine to ask the caller to hold for just one moment while you locate your information. This also gives you a little time to take a deep breath and gather your thoughts for the call.

TIP: *Smile when you begin to speak. You will sound better on the telephone.*

Now that you are speaking to your contacts by telephone, you want to make an appointment to see them in person. Offer to meet at their most convenient time. Pharmaceuticalsales.com suggests that you invite them to a breakfast or lunch meeting where you can talk one-on-one. Sales professionals are often too familiar with providing meals for their customers, and it can be a refreshing change to have someone buy them lunch. If they do not have time for a meal, perhaps a coffee break would work better. Have them choose the restaurant or coffee shop that would be convenient for them. Have several locations in mind in case they want you to pick the place.

You have made your appointment! You are on course and networking the pharmaceuticalsales.com way. Remember, this is your first interview with someone who can boost your career; be prepared. At this stage of the game, you will be controlling most of the dialogue. Review all of the information you have learned about the company (Chapter 4) and show your contact that you are familiar with their company. Your preparation will demonstrate that you are serious and committed. Your contact will not feel that you have wasted his time. On the contrary, he will be more likely to provide you with the information you want, and even the connection you want with a District or Division Manager.

When you meet, bring your resume and the other information you have collected to show your dedication. Write notes regarding what you want to say and ask. Be friendly and enthusiastic. Remember this individual can be a critical part of your job search. They will be evaluating you, wondering if you would be a good candidate to work with, and one that they can honestly recommend to their company. Most pharmaceutical companies pay a finder's fee to their own employees for candidates whom they recommend and are hired. If so, sales representatives will be on the lookout for good people!

The contact person with whom you are networking is representing their pharmaceutical organization. You are representing yourself. If you show up in attire that is inappropriate, your contact will probably conclude that you are not likely to demonstrate good judgment in their organization. Always dress the part (Chapter 3) in every networking situation.

Now, what kind of information do you want from your meetings and telephone calls with industry contacts? First, thank the person for meeting with you. State that you are excited about the career opportunities available in pharmaceutical sales and you would like to learn as much as possible about his or her job experience. You have two goals for the networking meeting. 1) Gain an understanding of the industry and this particular pharmaceutical organization. 2) Develop your relationship with the individual representative.

Getting to know representatives on the inside of the industry adds knowledge about the answer to this often asked question: "How did Janet Jones get that job with XYZ Pharmaceutical Company?" Answer: "She knew someone."

Have a list of questions that you can use for all your contacts. Twenty networking questions you might use are listed below. You will not ask all these questions at one meeting, of course, but tailor them to your interests with this particular organization. Be sensitive to the other person, do not bombard them with closed-ended questions. Instead, ask open-ended questions that will encourage them to discuss freely. Begin with questions that are more personal and show interest in the person. This will invite them to speak and builds rapport between you.

TWENTY SAMPLE QUESTIONS FOR YOUR INDUSTRY CONTACTS

1. What is your current job?
2. Why did you decide to enter a career in pharmaceutical sales?
3. How did you get your first job in pharmaceutical sales?

4. What educational background do you have? What is your job experience?

5. How did you obtain your current position with XYZ Pharmaceutical Company?

6. What do you like about your current position?

7. What, if anything, do you dislike?

8. What is a typical day like in your territory? Who are your customers (doctors, pharmacists, hospitals, clinics, etc.)? How many customers do you have?

9. Who is your competition in the marketplace? How many competitors do you have for your promoted products? How does your product rank in sales versus the competition?

10. How are your customers receiving your products?

11. What differentiates you from your competition?

12. How does your company measure sales performance?

13. What kind of training does your company provide?

14. How is your company structured? What are the various divisions? How is your company's sales force structured (districts, regions, business units, etc.)?

15. What new products does your company have in development? What new products are expected in the next twelve months? What are they indicated for, and what advantages do they have over competing products?

16. What are some career options that you have within your organization that may be of interest to you?

17. Do you know of other Pharmaceutical Representatives with other companies I could contact? Do you have their telephone numbers, business cards, or addresses?

18. Is there a local professional association of pharmaceutical sales representatives? Whom could I contact to see about attending a meeting?

19. Are there any open sales positions now or will there be in the near future? May I forward my resume to your District Manager? (Get name and address).

20. I am very interested in a career with XYZ Pharmaceutical Corporation. Will you please forward my resume to your district manager?

Conclude by thanking the individual for taking the time to meet with you. Ask if you may follow-up with a telephone call in four to six weeks to see if there are any positions open or possible opportunities in the future. Ask if he or she would contact you in the future if an opening even looks as if it might be available. It is to your advantage to know about it as soon as possible so you can respond quickly.

Now, what do you do? Complete your notes, adding information you learned to the Profile section of Insight. Always send a typed follow-up letter within 24 hours (see example at end of chapter). Managers state that if a candidate does not show this simple courtesy they will likely be eliminated from the interview process. If your contact has provided you with additional names and addresses within the company, such as a District Manager, make that connection as soon as possible.

If you learn about any industry associates with other companies, start a new file for that company, including a new worksheet. Make a note right away about how and from whom you received the contact information.

When you hear of an available position, move quickly! Express great interest in the position and ask for an interview. Get your resume to your contact person, and to the district manager, immediately. Use U.S. Postal Service Priority Mail or overnight delivery such as FedEx, which adds attention and urgency to it. Also, ask the representative if you may call the District Manager. If so, now is the time to get their telephone number and call them. Explain how you learned of the position and ask for the interview.

If you do not hear of any open positions right away, be patient. Your networking process will expand over time. Continue to make new contacts and meet more people every week. pharmaceutical-sales.com suggests that you make several initial telephone calls each day, which will lead to a growing number of appointments each week. Be confident that you are building your own success, and that over time you will gain the interviews and the job offer you are seeking. It may take several months or more of networking with your contacts. Some opportunities my come up even a year later. To maintain your relationship with your network, follow-up with telephone calls every four to six weeks. They will remember you and call you when there is an opportunity. With this strategy, you are placing yourself in front of other candidates. Only you can make it work. Stay focused and persistent. You will close the sale!

TIP: *Observe a Pharmaceutical Representative performing his or her job in real situations with real customers. Pharmaceuticalsales.com refers to this strategy as the "Pharmaceutical Career Preceptorship" (described below).*

District Managers want to hire an individual who is knowledgeable about the position for which they are interviewing. In other words, they want to know that you have researched the job thoroughly, you know what the job involves, and you are determined to get it. One way to demonstrate this is to show that experience on your resume in any other sales position. However, never put false information on your resume. State clearly that you want to work in a pharmaceutical sales position.

So how do you gain a level of experience that will set you apart from other candidates? We suggest that you spend time in the field observing other sales representatives. This is called a "pharmaceutical career preceptorship." To achieve success, ask one of your networking contacts to allow you to accompany him for a day or a few hours as he goes about his normal routine. You will see first hand what he does and says. After completing a pharmaceutical preceptorship, include it on your resume.

Not every representative will be open to this suggestion. If you are turned down, keep asking others. Be mindful that your acquaintance may need to check with his district manager first, and convey this understanding to your contact. Take whatever time is allotted for you. Since you may need to settle on half a day, or one or two call; try it with more than one contact, and go on more than one preceptorship if you can.

As you go through the day, observe everything you can about what the representative is doing, and why. Make notes at the end of the preceptorship. Be prepared to describe during your interview what you have done and include examples. This is an excellent way to show that you are committed to your career choice! You are taking it upon yourself to direct your learning and experience. It will truly get you noticed and set you apart.

TIP: *Keep yourself on "interviewing behavior" at all times. Picture yourself as a future employee or co-worker of the persons you are contacting and meeting.*

Now that you are actively networking and researching the industry, you are likely to get to your next step—the interview. Chapter 6 promises many insights into this exciting stage of attaining your career goal.

[SAMPLE LETTER: FOLLOW-UP NETWORKING MEETING]

May 25, 2002

Janet Lynn Jones
1234 Summer Boulevard
Winter, PA 19123

Ms. Nancy Young
XYZ Pharmaceutical Company Inc.
1134 W. Elm Street
Milentz, PA 19126

Dear Ms. Young:

It was a pleasure seeing you today. I value your making the time in your busy schedule to meet with me.

Your position in pharmaceutical sales sounds exciting. I will call the contacts you gave me, and I have scheduled myself to attend the Philadelphia Representative Association meeting next month.

XYZ Pharmaceutical Company seems like an excellent organization. I believe your new product for cholesterol will be a huge success in an extremely competitive market. I would like to have the opportunity to interview with XYZ. I appreciate you informing your district manager of my desire to enter this industry with your company. Should any territories become available, please contact me.

As we discussed, I will call you in four to six weeks. In the meantime, please call me if any opportunities arise. My home phone is 555-5555. Again, thank you for your time and assistance. I am looking forward to working with you in the future!

Sincerely,

Janet Lynn Jones

[SAMPLE LETTER: FOLLOW-UP PRECEPTORSHIP]

June 4, 2002

Janet Jones
1234 Summer Boulevard
Winter, PA 19123

William Brady
XYZ Pharmaceutical Company Inc.
1134 W. Elm Street
Milentz, PA 19134

Dear Mr. Brady:

I appreciate the time you spent this afternoon showing me aspects of your job with XYZ Pharmaceutical Company.

It was fascinating to see the consultative sales approach you use and how you schedule your day. Dr. Wellborn was interested in your new product for cholesterol and was eager to hear the points you made from the medical journal article.

Again, I would like to express my interest in any territories that become available with XYZ Pharmaceutical Company. I appreciate you informing your district manager of my determination to enter this industry. With your recommendation, I will forward my resume to him.

Thank you so much for your assistance. As we agreed, I will call you in four to six weeks to check on the status of any opportunities in your company. In the meantime, please call me if an opportunity develops. My home phone number is 555-5555.

Sincerely,

Janet Jones

Chapter 6

The Interview

As you successfully apply the networking strategies described by pharmaceuticalsales.com, you will soon be reaping the desired result—Interviews. The chapter you are about to read describes what you should expect from the interview process and how you should prepare for it. This approach helps you to be at your best, with the greatest level of confidence. Included at the end of the chapter is a list of guidelines for professional attire that will have you looking and feeling your professional best as well.

Your first meeting is potentially the beginning of a long-term relationship, therefore it is critical that you present a positive, winning image throughout the interview process. Initiate that relationship on your terms, and be the consummate professional.

Interviewing with pharmaceutical companies has its unique challenges. There are several different types of discussions you might experience with any given company. How you handle each of them is critical to your success. There will be a progression of meetings as you advance through the interviewing process. Be prepared for the various conversations you will have. Fortunately, your strategy will be essentially the same regardless of the type. However, there are some variations in how you must conduct yourself. Pharmaceuticalsales.com labels the different types of interviews as follows:

1. Screening Interview
2. Job Fairs
3. Initial, or first Interview
4. Second Interview
5. Final Interview

Companies and District Managers will vary in how they conduct each step. They will also differ in the type of questions they ask and the manner in which they ask them. This fact underscores your need to be prepared for anything since you may or may not be given prior advice regarding the types of questions you will be expected to answer. For example, some interviewers may ask questions consisting of situations that occur in the day-to-day work of the Pharmaceutical Representative. In some cases, you will be given the situations in order to prepare for either a telephone screening or a face-to-face interview. The situational questions could be customer-related or company-related. Customer related situations would be challenges that come up with doctors, office nurses, and receptionists or gatekeepers. They could also be objections to your product, such as having a higher cost than your competitor. Company-related situations are about working on teams with other representatives.

Because some companies are asking job-specific questions, it is important for you to study the answers in this guide. Also imperative is time in the field with a Sales Representative to observe what they do (this is a "field preceptorship" as discussed in Chapter 5). Perform the preceptorship early in your job search. Create a list of scenarios that you want to observe and use the situations Insight provides. Ask the representatives you talk and meet with how they would handle each one. You may add excellent and creative answers to your knowledge base.

Not every company will ask situational questions about selling pharmaceuticals. However, regardless of the situation or exact wording of the question, the interviewer is looking for evidence of whether or not you would be the right candidate for the job. Obviously, you have not had previous experience selling pharmaceuticals and the interviewer is aware of that. Initially they are looking for the way you think, how you sell, and what your skills are in different job competencies. Your answers should always include specific examples about how you were successful in similar situations, either current or past positions. This is critical. The interviewer will be looking for explicit behavior patterns and will ask if you do not provide them. One suggestion is to use a simple format to describe your accomplishments: Situation-Action-Results. Even if the question is about selling to doctors or other aspects of pharmaceutical sales, your answer should include a similar personal experience and detail how you handled it successfully.

Studying each question in this chapter will help you understand what the interviewer is trying to assess. Behind each question is an essential skill or behavior for successful performance on the job. The essential skills are usually called job "competencies," as listed and discussed in Chapter 2. To simplify competencies, they can be condensed into three categories that you should keep in mind as you develop and rehearse your answers:

Achievement drive: results oriented, creative, confident, history of sales success

Strong work ethic: motivation, reliability, communication

Positive attitude: flexibility, teamwork, high energy

SCREENING INTERVIEW

Screening interviews are conducted, to put it bluntly, in order reduce the number of candidates after the unacceptable resumes have been culled from the stack. They are designed to identify the general qualities, or profile, of the desired candidate. These dialogues are often conducted by telephone, but may also be done face-to-face. Several characteristics distinguish the screening interviews from other types. First, it is usually brief and lasts about twenty to thirty minutes. Second, someone may conduct it other than the District Manager (such as a Human Resources Specialist, Sales Trainer, or Hiring Agency). Finally, it is generally an identical set of questions for all candidates. A scoring system is used to determine who will advance to the first interview stage.

Screening interviews may not be scheduled ahead of time. You should be prepared for a call whenever you are actively networking. Keep your interview file close by and easily accessible at all times. Include your resume, job accomplishments, sales achievements, networking, and research notes that you have collected on each company.

TIP: *When the phone rings for a screening interview, feel free to ask the caller to wait just a moment, saying you would like to close the door, turn off the radio, get off the other line, let others at home know not to disturb you, or whatever. Take thirty seconds or so to gather your file and collect your thoughts. Then lift the receiver and thank the caller for waiting.*

If you have done your research and practiced your answers, you will sail past the screening step. Be sure to take notes. Write down the person's name and title immediately, and do not be afraid to ask for correct spelling of the name. You will need the address, fax, telephone number, and email address if they will give it to you. At the end, ask questions about the interview process, and close by requesting a face to face interview.

When you complete this phase, send a follow-up letter via fax or overnight mail. Emphasize your desire for the opportunity to demonstrate why you believe you will be a successful sales representative for the company.

JOB FAIRS

Job fairs are similar to screening interviews in that they are designed to eliminate lesser-qualified candidates. The interviewers are more likely to be Human Resource personnel, Sales Trainers, or District Managers from other areas. These individuals are not empowered to hire you, but can make a good case either for or against you. Approach and follow up with them as you would the District Manager.

One advantage of the job fair is that you are face to face immediately with the company personnel. Take the opportunity to set yourself apart. The questions they ask will most likely be standard for each candidate that allows the interviewer to use a scoring system and classification of candidates. Do not underestimate the importance of this part of the process. Have your file ready and your answers prepared. Again, close on getting to the next step. Collect as many business cards as there are people from the company—meet everybody, and follow up with each person.

INITIAL OR FIRST INTERVIEW

This is the real thing. Congratulations! You are probably one of five or ten candidates invited for a full interview. This is your first meeting with the District Manager, and it is the opportunity for you to become the top candidate. You will be asked specific questions, and be able to ask your own questions. Volunteer as much information about yourself as you can, and always include successful scenarios.

Most companies will allow one hour for the initial interview. Be prepared to go longer—this will be good sign that you are serious candidate. Otherwise, the manager would not spend the extra time with you. Some companies will arrange for more than one interview at this stage. You may interview with more than one DM, Sales Trainer, Regional Field Trainer, or even a Regional Manager (RM) if they are trying to move quickly to fill the position.

Always conduct yourself professionally with every individual you meet during this process. While waiting, secretaries to Regional Managers may address you, but you may not know one from the other. Be relaxed and confident. Converse briefly with them if you are given the opportunity, asking them topical questions such as who they are and what they do.

Have your own questions to ask the interviewer, but do not ask about compensation or benefits at the initial interview. There is more on this topic, including questions for you to ask, in Chapter 7.

SECOND INTERVIEW

Returning for a second interview means that you are considered a serious candidate. The questions asked will be more specific. There may be additional people involved, such as another DM or the RM. However, the second interview may only be with the same DM. Many DM's will not hire or advance a candidate to the final step unless they see that candidate more than once. This allows the DM to confirm or challenge conclusions made in the first interview.

FINAL INTERVIEW

Sometimes a third interview is necessary to answer a few remaining questions or to have someone else in the company meet you. You can be confident at this point that there are only two candidates left—you and one other. Sometimes this step takes place in a different setting, such as a restaurant. This allows the Manager to see how you conduct yourself in a less formal and controlled setting where you both can let your guard down. It permits them see more of your personality, and you to see more of theirs. This is where chemistry is important. So, be relaxed and confident. Be conversational but avoid controversial topics and banter. Be thoughtful, polite and positive in your comments at all times.

As in other steps of the process, close for the job offer. Review what has been agreed upon so far in terms of your qualifications. Ask if there is anything missing or still needed in order for the Manager to reach his or her decision. If so, provide it. Either way, close for the job clearly and with determination. A sale is about closing the deal.

Your preparation for the interview includes the networking and research strategies outlined in Chapters 4 and 5. In this chapter, pharmaceuticalsales.com provides the most common interview questions, and offers suggestions and examples of how you might answer each one. Give the finest response to every question based on your education, background, work experience, and the recommendations in this manual. Learn the questions from this chapter well because undoubtedly you will be asked some, if not all, of them. Prepare your answers ahead of time and practice your responses until you are comfortable with each one. Remember, the more organized you are, the more relaxed and confident you will be and the better you will perform.

TIP: *An excellent strategy is to tape record the questions and your responses. Play back your answer and re-record it until you are happy with it. Videotaping is also an excellent way to prepare yourself. Be your own critic! As you hear and see yourself, you will reveal areas that need improvement. Note your non-verbal behavior—such as your posture, tone of voice, and how well your voice is projecting. Do you look and sound confident? These practice sessions will give you a profound advantage over other candidates.*

As discussed in earlier chapters, know as much as you can about the company and determine how you see yourself adding value in the environment. Begin by telling the interviewer that you have researched the pharmaceutical industry, his or her company, and the job of pharmaceutical sales representative. If you have purchased a share of stock, do not forget to mention it. State firmly that you are extremely interested in the job. The interviewer, upon hearing such an aggressive opening, will often give you the opportunity to tell them what you know. This puts you in charge of the interview.

Sometimes you will discover that the interviewer is not exactly what you expected or were looking for in a Manager. You will find that occasionally they are not as prepared for the process as you are. When this is the case, you need to volunteer the answers you have prepared, even without being asked. Weave your accomplishments and strong points throughout the interview. Your confidence will show, and your skills and preparation will be rewarded.

The interviewer will be looking for initiative. Showing the strategy you used to network, research, and prepare yourself for this process is, in itself, evidence that you have initiative and are determined to succeed. Make the conclusion for the interviewer to see that you will apply the same skills and abilities that you brought to the interview process to your new career.

Pharmaceuticalsales.com has provided you the questions you may be asked. We have also included twenty questions that you may want to ask the interviewer. You should ask questions during every interview to show your interest. As you progress through the later stages of the process, such as in second and third interviews, ask more in depth questions than you would in a screening or initial interview. Why? Your original goal was to market yourself. You have their interest, but is the company a good match for you—ask questions. Do not, at any point in the process, ask about compensation or benefits. Get the offer first! There will be plenty of opportunity to discuss bonus payments and the dental plan after that.

TIP: *Before leaving the interview, be certain to obtain the interviewer's business card. You will need it for completing your follow-up correspondence (see sample letter at end of this chapter).*

THE MOST COMMON QUESTION FOR INTERVIEWING IN PHARMACEUTICAL SALES.

The following questions are typical of what you should expect during an interview. The interviewer will use variations, but by knowing the answers your responses will be appropriate and effective no matter how the questions are asked. Your preparation, including the industry and company-specific research, means you are ready for anything.

TIP: *You should never be asked certain questions. It is illegal for employers to inquire about certain areas of your life. However, you may volunteer any information you choose and the interviewer can listen to it once you bring it up, but they cannot ask for it. These questions include information about the following:*

- *marital status*
- *family*
- *religion*
- *age*
- *sexual preference*
- *race or national origin*
- *political affiliation*
- *arrest record; the exception is convictions*

- *height or weight*
- *emergency contact information*
- *type of military discharge*
- *health status*
- *to provide a photo*
- *children or the possibility of pregnancy*
- *spouse's vocation*
- *memberships in organizations, clubs, and societies*

You can be asked to list professional organizations, and this is an opportunity to expand their perception of you.

1) Why do you want to enter a career in pharmaceutical sales?

This is a fundamental question, and one you must be able to answer without hesitation. There are two parts to this question and it deserves a two-part answer. Why do you want to sell, and why in the pharmaceutical industry. State that you want and like to sell, and that you are successful at doing so. You possess the essential qualities of high energy, motivation, confidence, dedication, creativity, and organizational skills. Provide specific examples of situations that demonstrate one or more of these qualities.

Next, selling pharmaceuticals appeals to you because it is challenging and rewarding. The challenge lies in its technical environment (product knowledge), professional customer audience, and stiff competition. The rewards are based on your own individual efforts, which is just the type of environment in which you excel. Use the same examples you gave to illustrate essential sales qualities in the first part of your answer. Only this time, relate it to something you think you would do in your new position as a sales representative for XYZ Pharmaceutical Company.

TIP: *This question provides an excellent opportunity for you to describe your research into the pharmaceutical industry and specifically with XYZ Pharmaceuticals. Since you have networked with many sales representatives by this point, you can use specific examples gleaned from your conversations with them and real-life situations you have had in front of customers. Use your answer to highlight your industry exploration. This will give you credibility when you say you want the job—you know what you are getting into and it is the perfect fit for you.*

2) Why do you believe that you would find pharmaceutical sales a rewarding career?

You know from your extensive research of the job and the company that you would find this profession challenging. It will be apparent to the interviewer whether you have done your homework. Answers such as "I have a friend that likes it" will not be sufficient.

You may include that you like being responsible for you own destiny. You are aggressive. You work hard. You will succeed based on your own merit. Include an example from a previous selling or business success.

You may also include your knowledge of the career advancement opportunities, as described in Chapter 2. Communicate your excitement about the possibilities for personal and professional growth. State that you are willing to dedicate the time and effort to learn the business from the field sales position.

3) Why do you think you would excel at pharmaceutical sales?

This is a similar question to the two above, but by asking it, the interviewer is seeking more information. You should answer that you know what this position requires and you have those requirements. Give some specific qualities that you possess that are also critical for success in pharmaceuticals. For example, you have individual creativity—Pharmaceutical Representatives work alone and face unique challenges that require unique solutions. You possess excellent time management skills—a busy representative must plan and work efficiently. You have excellent business acumen, a skill that will help you target your most productive customers, which saves time and is more productive. Again, you are indicating that you know what the position entails.

Also, be sure to include the fact that you will enjoy it. If you are doing something that brings great pleasure and confidence, you will naturally do it better. Being happy in your work is a principal indicator of success, and that makes you sure that you are pursuing the right position.

4) How long do you believe you would like to sell pharmaceuticals?

Be sure you relate to the interviewer that as long as you feel challenged and rewarded by the position, you feel your time is unconstrained. If career advancement is one of your goals, communicate that you desire to learn the industry "from the entry sales position up." You plan to use the opportunity to develop your strengths and assess your opportunities as you add value to the company, then realistically evaluate your career goals at that time.

5) Why do you want to change careers to pharmaceutical sales?

This question is looking for your conviction about what you want to do. Think about what attracted you to pharmaceuticals and why you started researching. Prepare an honest answer and convey your excitement.

The pharmaceutical industry has much to offer. You may be looking for growth. This industry has shown compelling expansion in the past and is poised to continue to do so in the future. You may want security. This industry is virtually recession proof. You may want prestige. This industry is one of the most sought-after and well-heeled industries in the world. You may be looking for a mixture of business and health care. You may desire professional, consultative relationships with your customers where you are the expert.

Perhaps you are more idealistic. You may want to be part of scientific discoveries and medical advances that alleviate suffering and improve people's lives. You want to offer solutions to real-life problems that physicians and patients face every day.

Whatever the reason, deliver it with conviction.

6) What experience do you have that would lend itself to pharmaceutical sales?

If you have experience selling a product or service, this is the time to sell the interviewer on how you performed. If you have no previous sales experience, describe times in the past that you have sold an idea, a project, or a new way of doing things at your work or school.

Sales experience is not essential for entering the industry. If you conduct research, then network with individuals in the profession and convey your determination to be successful, you will be conclusively more desirable as a candidate than someone with sales experience who has not prepared as effectively as you have.

7) How does your education prepare you for a career in pharmaceutical sales?

Most any undergraduate college degree will easily lend itself to the industry.

Business, communications, marketing, management, education, language skills, psychology, biology, chemistry, pharmacy, nursing, and others, all enhance what you bring to this company. If your education is in science or health care, you are going to have to emphasize that you can "sell." If your background is sales, emphasize that you can learn the essential technical background needed to excel in this position.

Pharmaceutical sales are a union of science and business. Prepare your answers to incorporate your education into this union.

8) Why do want to work for XYZ Pharmaceutical Company?

The interviewer wants to know if you have done your homework. What are some unique characteristics of this company? Is it relatively large, small, or medium sized? What is its product line or area of medical specialty that you like? Are you excited about the current product line and the future possibilities of products to be released? Do you know anybody who works for the company? State that you are impressed with current pharmaceutical sales representatives that you have met through your networking, and that you would have an excellent working chemistry with the team.

TIP: *If you have done your research, you may even be more informed about this organization than the person on the other side of the table. See if you can surprise him with information he was not aware of, such as an experimental compound in development, or the latest quarterly profit figures. Managers will often be unaware of some details about their company because they are more involved with the day to day business of their district.*

9) What qualifies you to be a Pharmaceutical Sales Representative?

If you have obtained a four-year degree, are interested, have completed the research, networked with individuals, understand the position and the industry, and most importantly, want to do this job, you are qualified. However, the interviewer is looking for more. Emphasize to the interviewer that you want to make a long-term commitment to this industry based upon your research. You have devoted countless hours of time and energy towards obtaining your goal, which is employment in this business. You plan to be well versed in product knowledge, selling skills, and territory organization. You want to excel and will bring value to the company.

10) Are you currently interviewing with other pharmaceutical companies at this time?

You want to work in pharmaceutical sales. It is as simple as that, so be honest. State that your goal is to gain successful employment with a dynamic pharmaceutical company, and that you will persist until you accomplish your goal. Describe your networking strategy. Include that you are, or will be, interviewing with prospective companies as you push to uncover opportunities.

If this is your first interview, state that. However, if you are currently interviewing with other companies make it clear. Include companies by name, names of individuals with whom you have met or interviewed, and a major product or two made by the other companies.

TIP: *Ninety percent of the candidates interviewing today cannot state what current products are being promoted by the firm they are interviewing with, much less the products of other* *companies. Think of the advantage you will create for yourself with this prospective employer by being versed on multiple companies in the industry.*

11) What are your greatest strengths?

Make sure that you can answer this question. It was probably used on the first interview in history. You will probably be presented with this query every time you interview in your working career.

Your strengths should be qualities that are in demand by pharmaceutical companies. You want to fit the profile of the successful representative by following the pharmaceuticalsales.com way.

- Self-motivated and self-disciplined: Your time management and organizational skills make you pro ductive while working autonomously or with little supervision.
- Creative: You are able to differentiate yourself from other pharmaceutical sales representatives. You can create ways to access your "hard to see" doctors.
- Goal oriented: You do what it takes to get the job done, including making a few extra calls to physi cians, hospitals, and pharmacies.
- Confident: Your background, qualities, and commitment will guarantee success in this career choice.
- Flexible: You are cooperative—you can take direction well, and work together as a team to reach corporate objectives.

12) What are your weaknesses? In what areas would you like to improve?

This question usually follows the one about strengths. Design your response so that ultimately your weakness is strength. Your interviewer will probably know what you are doing, but the fact that you have done the preparation to handle this difficult question will gain their respect. They are looking for your confidence under pressure. Many of your contemporaries will struggle with this question. Poor answers are ones that shift the weakness to another person, such as a previous manager, co-workers, or company policy. Be careful not to interject blame or negative comments about past employers and others.

Two examples of a good answer are as follows:

- Sometimes I have trouble compiling my paperwork in an enthusiastic manner. However, I do know that timeliness of reporting is important to my managers and my company, so I make sure I am always prompt with its delivery.
- Sometimes I have difficulty when other individuals do not display a positive attitude towards new ideas. I make it a point to stay positive, hoping it will influence other members of the organization or team.

13) Where do you see yourself five years from now?

From your research, you know that there are many opportunities in the pharmaceutical industry for a successful field representative: Management, Marketing, Sales Training, Sales Support, Communications, Professional Education. Reiterate that learning the field sales position and becoming a proven performer within your organization is your primary goal for at least the next three years. After learning the business from this level, you will direct your goals so that you can grow the most profes-sionally and contribute to the corporations' goals.

TIP: *During the initial phases of interviewing, most District Managers will delight in hearing that you are giving yourself three to five years to fully develop and demonstrate your abilities in your new territory. It is a sign of unrealistic expectations and poor knowledge of the job when a candidate places too much emphasis on upward mobility when they have not even entered the industry. Show your ambition in other ways—by researching, networking, preparing, and inter viewing with excellence.*

14) How do you feel about your current boss?

If you do not get along with your current boss, this is not the time to voice it. State that you have been managed effectively, provided guidance, and growth in your position. Specify that you have met your objectives, but do not talk about personalities and philosophies. As long as you perform your job, and reach or surpass your objectives, you feel just great about your current boss.

15) How do you feel about your current employer?

Again, never complain about your present position. State that the position has provided you with the ability to gain knowledge and grow professionally, but you desire a personal and professional challenge. Considering your research and career planning, the ideal career for you is in the pharmaceutical industry. Talk less about your current position and more about your decision to become a pharmaceutical sales representative. Keep your answer positive and career oriented. In other words, show that you are moving towards pharmaceuticals, not moving away from some other situation that you do not like.

16) What have you done that shows initiative in your present position?

Use a recent example in your present position, if possible, to describe the details of your current position. Your pharmaceutical research also provides an excellent response.

17) What are your immediate goals?

Your immediate goals are both professional and personal. Articulate that your number one professional priority is to achieve a career with a pharmaceutical company and begin contributing as a successful representative. Add personal goals, such as physical exercise, hobbies, family, if you would like, to round out this response.

18) What are your interest, hobbies?

Choose activities that show competition, determination, motivation, creativity, or team playing. These attributes are the ones that fit the profile of success, and transfer well to the job. Leave out watching television, going to the movies, reading, and other sedentary activities.

19) Describe a problem you have encountered in your current position?

The interviewer is really looking for a solution you created. Thus, you must not only describe a problem, but also describe a solution to the problem. Example: "A problem in my current position was that we were unable to reach some of the deadlines of our department. I overcame this by placing a large calendar in the break room with our deadlines marked in red. It was a clear reminder to the other office members, which in turn improved hitting our deadlines."

20) What have been some of your largest disappointments?

Describe a situation where you experienced disappointment and were able to learn and develop from it, thus turning it into a positive experience. Example: "As I began my job search in the pharmaceutical industry I found that it was taking too long to get my first interview. Since then, I have changed my approach and become more aggressive at discovering opportunities. Therefore, I have become much more successful. I feel most disappointments can teach us something useful for the future."

21) How do you prepare your reports or paperwork in your current position?

Example: "I create my reports to communicate relevant information about my business. Not only for my manager and my company, but also for myself. I find they are more useful when I write them as soon as I complete a sales call. I make sure that my reports are prompt, organized, and detailed, yet concise."

22) Have you ever had to deal with a difficult person at work? How did you handle this?

If you have never done so, then say that and be finished with the question. If you have, describe a situation in which, though you did not agree with an individual, you where able to work through the assignment or task to complete the project. It is more important to cooperate with individuals so that the work atmosphere remains productive.

23) Do you feel you are treated and compensated fairly at your present position?

Never complain about your present position, boss, company, duties, etc. The interviewer wants to know you are a positive force. Simply answer, "Yes."

24) What is your largest accomplishment in your present position?

If you have received any awards or commendations, mention them. Bring documentation of any recognition that you have been awarded, and show it to the interviewer. Describe a work situation that you resolved with favorable results, or a creative solution you used with a difficult customer. Although the question may be worded specifically to address your present position, take license to expand to other jobs or to extracurricular or community accomplishments, as well.

TIP: *Use your answers to lead the interviewer to other areas you would like to present about yourself. Find a way to bridge to another topic or example that you know is a positive attribute for you. If you rely on the interviewer to ask the question, it may not be asked, and you will lose an opportunity to say something important about your successes.*

25) What do you dislike about your present position?

You may want to choose some minor and menial aspect of your job. It is a good idea to pick something that deters or distracts from the business. Office chatter is a good one, waiting on people who are late, or being stuck in traffic. Be sure to include what you do to deal with the problem. Paperwork is always a good thing to dislike. Just be sure to include that because you dislike it, you are sure to complete it in a timely and accurate way.

Conclude by saying that you have been satisfied with your present position, but you desire to accelerate your growth in pharmaceutical sales.

26) Do you feel you have been evaluated fairly?

Again, never complain about current or past positions. The interviewer is not looking for some-one who is unhappy in relationships with an employer, regardless of who is at fault. Do not complain about anything or blame anyone. A simple "yes" is appropriate.

27) Give me an example of one of your best sales.

If you are currently selling a product or service, use a sale in which you encountered objections, misunderstandings, or a lack of customer interest, and how you overcame these obstacles. If you are not currently selling a product or service, detail the way you have gone about marketing yourself through the interview process. Describe, in detail, how you have set goals, strategies, networked with individuals, and kept records. Compare the interviewing process to a sale. Express in either situation how rewarding your sales activity and accomplishing your goals was. Example: You have felt rewarded by your increased knowledge of the pharmaceutical industry and the people who work in it. You are confident you will be successful.

28) Give me an example of a sale that you missed, and how you could have handled it differently?

Failure is universal in sales. A good salesperson thrives on it. It is common for sales professionals to experience this, and the interviewer wants to know how you will respond to it when it happens again. Give an example, be honest, state what you learned in the process, and how you tried to correct the situation. If you have no sales experience, use a business or office situation in which you created a solution and benefited from a past failure. Either way, convey your excitement over challenging sales situations, customers, and the thrill of overcoming.

29) How do you go about selling your product?

Describe your sales cycle and approach to the customer. Do you initially use telephone contacts, direct mail, or any type of advertising? Be competent in your description of your sales process and how you differentiate yourself from your competition. Example: You telephone all customers within two weeks of their purchases to check their satisfaction with your product or service. This process has led to many repeat purchases of your product line, and improvements in your service.

30) Do you believe you are able to handle the pressure of sales quotas?

Yes. State that you find the challenge of sales quotas motivating. You enjoy being responsible for your own destiny. You work hard and want to be recognized and compensated according to what you accomplish.

31) How do you handle rejection in your sales position?

Whether in the sales position or your current career search you must often experience some rejections before success. Rejection is an opportunity to get to know your customer better. It forces you to make changes in your approach. Creating innovative solutions has provided ways that have allowed you to move closer to your customers and understand them better.

32) What things do you and your current manager disagree on?

State that you and your manager rarely have disagreed on issues, and that your relationship has been very productive within your organization.

33) How are you motivated in your position?

This question tells the interviewer what you will be like to manage. You are motivated by a job well done. Your own accomplishment and success feeds you. Besides being self-motivated, you thrive on recognition from within your company, comments from your superiors with periodic performance reviews, and financial rewards (commission, bonuses, etc.). Also, state that you gain a sense of satisfaction by achieving personal goals. Example: To be in the top 10% of your company's sales force.

34) What things detract from some of your initiatives?

With this question, make a negative a positive. For example, you may occasionally overachieve. While good for the business, it can be better to keep a balance between your work and relaxation. You find that you are more productive when you take an occasional break to refocus.

35) How have you differentiated yourself from your peers both outside and within your organization?

Embellish the successful attributes of a salesperson: ambition, determination, organization, energy, self-motivation, ability to handle rejection, targeting the correct customer base, teamwork, etc. Give an example of a situation in which you excelled. Was there a time when you went the extra mile to help a customer? Perhaps your forte is personal rapport and relationship selling, or maybe you have a unique talent that you incorporate into your sales approach, such as cooking, fishing, or athletics?

36) How were your grades in college?

If they were admirable, bring an official transcript from your college or university to present to the interviewer. Your answer should focus on the fact that you will learn product knowledge quickly, and communicate that information to your customer. If grades were not praiseworthy, fault it on working while attending school (if appropriate), extracurricular activities (sports), or youth. Move on to illustrate recent successes in your career, continuing education, seminars, or training classes.

37) What is your current salary?

Answer briefly and to the point, then stop talking. Do not exaggerate. From your research, you know the starting salary range for a pharmaceutical sales representative. Avoid discussing what salary you may require until you have been made an offer. Likewise, avoid the temptation to ask anything about salary or compensation.

38) Can I contact your current employer, or co-workers?

"No" is an acceptable answer. You would not want to jeopardize your current standing within your present organization. Do offer references, both business and personal, and contact information for co-workers if acceptable to you.

TIP: *Do not bring pre-written reference letters. They are not of value to a prospective employer and may be insulting to the interviewer, especially if they are overstated (which most of them are). If it is appropriate in your situation to provide references, bring them type-written on a separate sheet of paper. Provide both personal and professional references; usually three of each is appropriate. Give complete names, titles, addresses, and telephone numbers. Be sure to have permission from the individuals on your list and keep them posted when you give out the list.*

39) When I call your references, how will they describe you? What would your boss say about you?

List some of the qualities that you have demonstrated for your referenced individuals. For example, they would say that you are determined to enter pharmaceutical sales, are creative and motivated, have a strong work ethic, are honest, reliable, good sense of humor, great salesperson, etc. Again, be sure you contact every one of your references before you list them. Let them know about your career search.

40) How much are you willing to travel? Are you willing to relocate?

Various positions or sales territories require that you travel, especially in the pharmaceutical industry. Even if you do not have to stay overnight to work your territory, you will surely have to travel to meetings, and training activities from time to time.

Your foremost consideration at this stage of the game is to obtain the job offer. Once you have an offer securely in hand, you can decide if the particulars of the position (travel, relocation, salary, benefits, commission structure, or management style) are satisfactory for you. Do not eliminate yourself from the process before receiving the offer you deserve. Always indicate that you are willing to travel and relocate for the right opportunity.

41) What do you expect to earn in the first year?

Never discuss salary until you have the offer in your hand. If you have done your research, you know the compensation level you can expect. Again, do not eliminate yourself by quoting too high, or even too low, a figure. State that you are confident that you will be compensated fairly for your efforts and you are looking forward to receiving an offer.

42) Describe what you believe a typical day, as a Pharmaceutical Representative, would involve?

This is your ideal question. Because of your networking, your field preceptorship, and other research, you are an expert at this question. Example: "Typically, an office based Pharmaceutical Representatives will start the day by stocking the trunk of the car with literature and samples. S/he will have a detailed plan for the day of where to go and who the contact is. A salesperson will call on 7-9 physicians to make detailed sales presentations. This may include visiting several pharmacies to gather information about prescribing habits and to check product supplies. Additionally, stopping at a hospital or clinic to reach physicians may be an alternative to their offices. The professional representative will assess how each physician is reacting to their product, present new information, leave samples, and get a commitment from the doctor for increasing prescriptions of the medication. During the office call, talking with the nurses, secretaries, and other office staff is an important part of communications.

Be sure to add a real-life example: "When I was observing Steve Brady for a day, we went to a new physician in the area and..."

43) How could you target the customers (physicians) in your territory in the most efficient way and still achieve maximum sales results?

This is a very advanced question and, if asked, means you are a serious contender. The more insight you can show about the job, the better. Answers that come from your own successes and networking are best, but we have included a few examples.

"Targeting" means choosing which doctors you are going to visit to make your sales presentations. This is your customer base. These doctors make up your call plan, as discussed in Chapter 2. Obviously, you cannot see all of the specialists in your territory. Many companies use call plans that are developed by the company or by consultants using sophisticated marketing data. Your call plan is then provided to you. However, it is usually not set in stone, and you are responsible for refining it based on your own observations in the field. The following answers are applicable to this process, and to the process of developing your own call plan.

First, match the product class to the physician's specialty. Example: You would call on a gynecologist more frequently to sell an oral contraceptive agent than you would to an internal medicine or general practice physician.

Second, evaluate the physician's practice size. Is their office busy? Do they see many patients of the type that would use your product? You can determine this by the number of patients waiting to be seen, number of support staff in the office (nurses and receptionist), or how full the appointment book is for the week. You would increase the number of calls to these physicians to promote their prescribing. This is "call frequency" and it is dependent upon the number of times you would normally call on that customer in a given time frame, referred to as "call cycle." Call cycle is the length of time you spend covering all locations in your territory one time. The company usually sets the call cycle. It can range from two weeks to two months, depending on territory size and sales strategy.

TIP: *Familiarize yourself with the terms such as targeting, call plan, call frequency, and call cycle. Review Chapter 2 for more information.*

For efficiency, plan your appointments by geography in your territory, and for the best times to see doctors without having to wait too long. Avoid walking in at busy times of the day. You will get to know this as you work a territory, and become more efficient as you learn about each customer and how the office runs.

44) What aspects of pharmaceutical sales do you feel are most vital to success in this field?

You can take your pick of the following suggestions or build your own list. The more relevant to your experience from discussions with your networking contacts, the better you will be. Examples: building customer relationships, being an expert on your products and the competition, listening for what the physician wants in a product and positioning your product accordingly, prompt follow-up, self-motivation, organization, creativity, determination, product knowledge, professionalism, and targeting your market.

45) What interests you least about the Pharmaceutical Sales Representative position?

Example: "I have done plenty of networking in the area of pharmaceutical sales, and I have not encountered anything I consider is a negative. Some Pharmaceutical Representatives that I have networked with have commented about waiting to see physicians, or the paperwork, or parking. I understand that these are all parts of the job, and there is a positive way to manage it, such as using downtime in waiting rooms to increase my product knowledge."

46) Let us pretend your product is a pen. Sell it to me.

Begin by probing the interviewer for requirements he or she is looking for in a pen. For example, "Why are you looking for a pen?" or "What are you looking for in a pen?" Listen and clarify the answer, then provide features and benefits of the pen that satisfy the stated need. Close the sale by asking for the business.

Feature	Benefit
• Round	• Easy to hold
• Shirt Clip	• Easy to find during daily activities
• Retractable point	• Will not leave marks on clothing
• Refillable cartridge	• Will provide years of service
• Smooth writing tip	• Effortless writing

Explore any reason that he or she would not want to use this pen. Close with, "How many would you like to order today?"

47) Let us pretend your product is XYZ Aspirin. Sell it to me.

Again, be certain to investigate what the customer would like to see in an ideal aspirin product. Listen, clarify, provide features and benefits, check for any questions or objections, and then ask for the business.

Feature	Benefit
• Low cost therapy	• Patient has more money for other things
• Pain relief in thirty minutes	• Patient can quickly resume normal activities
• Proven medication	• Doctor can prescribe it with confidence
• Low incidence of side effects	• Doctor will not be bothered by telephone calls from patients about side effects

Next prompt for acceptance: "Doctor, is there any reason you would not prescribe XYZ aspirin for your next patient with mild pain?"

Then close: "Will you prescribe XYZ aspirin to all of your patients today with mild pain?"

Of course, there are many ways you could finesse or alter the above selling situations. Each describe what you should explore first, listen carefully, present features and benefits, urge for acceptance, and close.

TIP: *Clip and save prescription drug advertisements from magazines. Medical journals are the best source for this information, but with DTC advertising, information is much more available. Find an advertisement for a medication manufactured by the company with which you are interviewing. Bring the article to the interview and make a sales presentation to the interviewer based on the advertised product. Use the advertisements as your sales "visual aid," and make a product presentation as if you were talking with a doctor. Be sure to practice ahead of time, and ask for coaching from an experienced pharmaceutical representative, if possible. Get the commitment from "the customer" to prescribe your "product."*

48) Respond to a physician stating, "Your product is too expensive."

"Cost is a common objection in sales, and is relative to the perceived value of the product. I believe with excellent product knowledge and persuasive selling skills, I would highlight the features and benefits of the medication over competitive therapies, and increase the value of the product in the physician's eyes. The best medication at the best price—that's a bargain!"

49) How do you believe you would develop your knowledge of a physician's needs in prescribing a drug therapy?

The interviewer is not looking for any one specific answer, but wants to see your poise, confidence, and sales skills. Obviously, if you have not worked in pharmaceutical sales, you will not have detailed answers. However, your industry research will give you some solid answers.

Example: "Listening, as in all sales, is the tool to uncover the needs of the customer (physician). Often, the customer will volunteer information, or offer open-ended questions that help me clarify my comments to increase his knowledge. I may also assume that many needs are common to many physicians and begin by addressing one specifically."

50) How would you deal with an angry receptionist or nurse in the physician's office, who was preventing you from seeing the physician?

In this situation, it is best to exhibit empathy. If an office is busy, as is common, it may mean that you have to return at a more opportune time. State that you understand the situation and request a better time for you to call back that day or that week. Sometimes, as in all sales, a client may take out their job frustration on a sales representative. You will show great sales maturity when you can diffuse such a situation and not take it personally. You are developing a long-term relationship. The customer is always right!

51) Tell me about a time you have failed.

This question and many like it are seeking information about what may appear to be negative answers. Be aware of the concept of "balance" during an interview. If an interview is going very well and the interviewer is beginning to believe you are a qualified candidate, he or she may start looking for balance. They will do this by looking for the human side of you, and this is a step forward. Your response helps them avoid concluding that you are "too good to be true," which could create a letdown for the manager after you are hired. It is okay to be human with your answers, and provide an example of when you feel you have failed. Make it a job-related answer, not personal. Also, incorporate how you dealt with the failure and how you learned to turn it into success.

52) How would you differentiate yourself among the many sales representatives calling on the same doctor?

This question is seeking creativity and familiarity with the daily role of the sales representative. First of all, use something about yourself that already makes you stand out—sense of humor, clinical or technical expertise, an avocation that can be shared such as cooking or golf. Then choose a solid skill necessary for top performance such as product knowledge—you will set yourself apart by providing value; also mention your excellent follow through on commitments, questions, etc.

53) How do you handle change on the job?

This question is looking for a healthy attitude towards the only constant in any pharmaceutical position—change! If you do not work well with change, you are interviewing for the wrong job. To answer this question successfully, as with all your responses, include an example of when and how you were confronted with a change and the way you handled it. Common changes you will encounter in pharmaceuticals (and almost any sales role) can vary from realignments in territories, to new products or products being pulled from the market, sales teams, managers, computer systems, sampling regulations and even company mergers. Your best attitude is that change is healthy and good; your approach is to always discern what you can and cannot control; always take a long-term view; set a good example for your colleagues by keeping them on track, too. Successful representatives stay focused on goals and opportunities. This requires flexibility and resilience; qualities that are also crucial for managers. You will be remembered for your abilities to work successfully in a constantly changing environment.

54) What would you do to get more time in front of busy doctors?

This is a good question to test your knowledge of the customer. Nine out of ten sales calls last less than two minutes. That job fact is not likely to change. You will need to follow two different directions with your answer. First, acknowledge that you know sales calls to physicians are less than two minutes and some are actually only a few seconds. This is not the end of the world, however, because doctors do everything quickly. They spend short periods multi-tasking, and are used to getting and giving information quickly and clearly. You must always be prepared to deliver your sales messages in the same manner. That takes excellent product knowledge and lots of practice. Try to extend the time of the call by presenting information the physician needs; this requires knowledge of that doctor's specific needs for his clientele, or by asking an engaging question on the disease or therapy you would like them to focus on at that time.

55) Sales Reps spend a good portion of the day behind the wheel. What would you do with that time?

This question will assess your organization and planning skills, self-motivation, and self-improvement skills. The obvious answer is listening to product or sales motivation tapes to educate yourself on the job, products, and selling skills. A good example would be CMR courses (Certified Medical Representative). You should include the obvious, but also set yourself apart by including this approach: efficient management of the territory to reduce windshield time. By taking time to plan each week and each day, you will know where to go and when to make best use of your own time and cut down on time spent in traffic.

56) How do you balance your work and family or non-work activities?

This question is looking for planning, setting goals, and prioritization. The pharmaceutical sales position requires 8-10 calls per day plus planning time, follow-up letters and memos, administrative reporting, etc. Your time selling is only part of the situation. For many representatives, this means working at home in the evenings at the expense of family or personal time. You will probably already have your own strategies for managing your off time. In addition, make the point that you prioritize what you need to do versus less critical activities. Though selling time is top priority, you also take advantage of downtime during the day to complete tasks. You do this by bringing materials such as clinical reprints to study while waiting in offices. You use your computer at lunch to complete memos or reports. You keep current with tasks so you do not fall behind. Therefore, you are free to enjoy your family time without being burdened by unfinished work.

57) How do you develop relationships with your customers?

The best approach is understanding and trust. Personal relationships are built on these precepts just as business and customer relationships are. Learn as much as you can about your customer's business, and about them personally; this is the best way to understand and address their needs. To develop trust, you always keep commitments and you provide objective information. That may mean including the negative aspects of your product. You do not emphasize negatives, but fair balance is especially important with pharmaceutical products. Your customer knows there are downsides to virtually all medications and still prescribes them. They need to know what to watch for and this will go a long way to gain their trust. In your answer, include an example of how you learn about your customers (what questions you ask, research you do, etc.) and a time when you gave fair balance about your product in a sales presentation.

58) How do you work on teams?

This question can take many forms, but the answer is always regarding how you work with others and manage team conflict. It is vital for Pharmaceutical Representatives to work well on teams because so many products are co-promoted by other representatives, divisions within your company, or even by other companies. This requires excellent communication and coordination. Your answer must include an example of how you demonstrated team skills:

• Respect the differences in others.

• Everyone does not approach the job the same way.

• Identify each person's goals.

• Realize their goals are often not the same, and may even conflict, with the job.

• State how you develop a common team goal on which to focus.

• Recognize individual goals including establishing dialog and agreed upon methods of communication such as meetings, email, voice mail, conference calls, etc.

• Resolve conflict.

• Use specific situations.

59) What do you think is the most important factor for success as a Pharmaceutical Rep?

This is the type of question that is looking for your level of knowledge and understanding of the position. As a side note, people generally answer this with an aspect of the job that they themselves do well. This is not necessarily a conscious process, and most managers are not aware of this connection. For the manager in the know, however, this question can be a way to identify what you consider your strength to be. There is no silver bullet answer for this one. Safe answers would be any of the core competencies listed in this guide. For example, "focus on results," or "positive attitude," or "knowledge of your products and customers" will be fine. As you give your answer, preempt the next logical question by also explaining why you chose that factor as the most important. Give an example of how you demonstrated that behavior in a current or previous job.

60) What do you expect the hardest part of being a Pharmaceutical Rep will be?

This question is looking for job knowledge first, and whether you know enough about the job to imagine what the biggest challenge would be. It also gives an indication of where you might have a developmental requirement that the manager will want to address in the future. That is not necessarily a negative—just more information the manager needs for the decision. Everyone has strengths and weaknesses and the manager seeks to identify these in serious candidates. The safe answer is, "access to the doctor," but follow your answer with ideas or what you would do to gain access to the doctor. Insight has previously provided answers to this question.

61) If a competitor moves your samples, what should you do?

Consult the nurse or office manager, whoever is in charge of the drug sample closet. State that your samples have been moved and ask for their suggestions as to what to do about it. Do not jump to conclusions that it was a competitor, even if you believe that is the case. Allow the office personnel to offer information since it may have been the staff or the doctor who moved your samples. Do not explicitly badmouth a competitor. This strategy will often result in the office personnel taking your side and providing a solution that will help you sell the most. It will also allow you to have more selling time during this process, and your professionalism will be highly regarded and you will be remembered for it.

62) A nurse or physician gets angry with you and says they are too busy to see you. What do you do?
Because this is a long-term relationship, you should remind yourself that everyone is allowed to have a bad day at the office. In a professional tone, agree that their schedules can be hectic and offer to return at a more convenient time. Although you may have already been waiting a long time, showing poise in

this situation makes you very welcome in the office. Being confrontational will aggravate the customer. When offering to return, you can often end up having more time with the doctor because they will remember that they made a commitment to see you later. You should also try to set an actual appointment. Appointment or not, it will be harder for them to turn you away the next time. Of course, when you return, you would remind them that they had suggested this was the best time to come back.

TIP: *You may be asked to describe what you would do in a very specific on-the-job situation for which you have no basis for an answer—because you are not yet a Pharmaceutical Rep. You can remain calm, buy time to think, and appear very professional. As a preface or introduction to your best guess answer, you will score extra points by starting off with the honest truth—that you are not sure how to answer an industry-specific question. The interviewer and you both know that you are not a Pharmaceutical Sales Representative and have no actual first-hand knowledge of the job. Therefore, you might begin the answer as follows, "As a new Representative, I may not be certain what to do in this situation. I would consult my manager or trainer if necessary before getting back to the customer with a correct response. Because you asked, here is one approach that I think would work, given the scenario you are describing." Then continue with your best response to the scenario.*

63) After meeting a doctor for the first time, thanking him for seeing you and introducing yourself, what next?

This question is looking for customer focus and selling skills. To answer it, describe the steps you take to understand the customer and establish trust. Even before establishing product needs, what is the best way to serve that individual in the long-term relationship? Determine the personality of the physician (such as talkative and friendly versus technically oriented) and use the correct approach. Once you learn the right tactic, you will want to know more about the physician's practice of medicine in the areas of your products. Ask a series of questions (sales probes) to see what they prescribe for the various disease states for which your products are indicated. Why do they make those choices? Answers may include efficacy, side effect profile (safety), price, managed care recommendations, etc.

Only after that process will you know the best manner and which specific information to present on your products. Always state that you will add any suggestions from your trainer/manager to your selling techniques.

64) What would you do after entering a doctor's office for the first time and introducing yourself to receptionist, if you are that told the staff of physician does not see sales representatives?

The manager is looking for your thought process as you evaluate and plan in this situation. This is more important than the specific answer. Focus your answer on how you would gather information and determine a course of action.

First, you have to know why you went into that office. Based on your pre-call planning (from prescription data, notes from previous representatives, etc.), is this a valuable target? Are you prospecting a potential target just because you are in the area? Next, you should get more information from the office to better plan your strategy for this doctor. Inquire about the policy. Have they seen representatives in the past? Is this a new policy? Why did it change? Are there any suggestions they will offer in terms of how to best reach the physician? Ask about when and where the doctor makes hospital rounds. Ask how he prefers to obtain information about drug products, and how he meets his continuing medical education requirements.

Once you leave the office, decide whether this physician can have an impact on your territory and what actions are appropriate to gain access to him. You should tap into your resources—ask experienced representatives, successful representatives, and your manager for ideas and tactics they have used. This may include seeing doctors outside the office, such as at the hospital. You may decide to provide product literature, clinical reprints, studies, and samples without seeing the doctor—using creative ways to call attention to it. You may also use mailings, educational programs, and entertainment events. Or you may discover that this physician has a very low potential for your products and remove them from your call list. Either way, research and due diligence is required on your part.

65) During your first month on the job, you meet with a doctor who just recently switched to competitor's product. How do you persuade him/her to come back to your product?

This is simple! Go back to the basics. Approach this doctor as you would any new customer and understand why the physician switched. Was it efficacy, safety, price, MCO recommendations? It may be as straightforward as the lack of a sales representative calling on them to provide needed services such as starter samples and updated information on the product. You will have to gain the physician's trust that you will take good care of your new client.

66) When presented with a last minute, unavoidable change to your itinerary, such as preparing for a new product launch, what planning, and coordination would you undertake to ensure nothing is missed?

This comes down to solid time management to make sure that you meet your commitments. You may have to work extra hard for a week making extra calls to cover your territory and keep up with new responsibilities. State that you are willing to make these calls in the early morning or evening if appropriate. Use time in the car and during one or two evenings or weekends to study. You may possibly even see some physicians on a Saturday morning. The interviewer wants to know how you can handle a little work pressure so show them that it would not phase you, that you have the commitment to your territory, and product knowledge to be a top performer. You would also talk it over with your manager and other team members to assist in setting appropriate goals and priorities.

67) You go to one of your regular doctor's offices and are introduced to a new physician who has just joined the practice. How do you approach the new doctor?

Introduce yourself with a handshake and present your card. Then use the same approach as any new customer—probe to develop an understanding of the doctor's preferences in how you can best be of service to her with her specific interests, personality, or behavioral style in mind. Understanding the doctor may include researching information regarding her background, when and how she prefers to see reps, and her attitude towards your products. Then go into a sales presentation that describes features and benefits, and reply to her concerns or objections, and when ready, close the sale.

68) A doctor tells you he will not prescribe your product because its cost is $10 more than your competitor's. What do you do?

The obvious answer to the cost objection is to clarify misunderstandings the customer may have on this issue including managed care formulary and reimbursement data. If the doctor has this information correct and you are dealing with a true cost objection, the next step is to outweigh it using patient and physician benefits of the product as well as with the service you provide. The cost of a product is relative to its perceived value. Highlight the features and benefits of this product as compared to the competition to demonstrate that while your product may cost more in the short term, it is ultimately a more cost effective way of treating patients overall.

69) It is your first week on the job. How do you get to see the doctors who are a priority?

At this point, the list of priority doctors is based on a territory analysis list. First, plan your day to have all the tools and supplies necessary to be effective. Next, map out the most efficient route to make the best use of your time. Consult your counterparts and manager for any advice as to the office protocol of these priority doctors. Once at an office, introduce yourself to the nurse or receptionist presenting them with your card and the name of your products. Probe for office protocol and any other information that would be important, and then ask specifically to see the doctor. If it is not possible to see the doctor at that time, arrange the best time to return and follow through exactly as agreed upon.

70) You are on a team with four other sales representatives. For the past few weeks, you have done all the planning of lunch meetings with the doctors. In your opinion, your teammates are not doing their share of the work. What do you do?

This is a common question that is similar to "How well do you work on teams?" First, bring it to the attention of your teammates and get their perception of the situation as you work out a solution. It may be a simple matter of asking for more help from them. If that does not bring about a resolution, the next step would be to take it to the attention of your manager for advice. There may be something going on that you are not aware of which is preventing the others on your team from assisting you with lunch meetings. Realize that you may have set a higher standard of expectations for yourself. Lead by example.

71) Why are you thinking of leaving your current position?

This question is looking for what motivates you and your level of knowledge about the Pharmaceutical Rep position. Include positive statements that indicate your desire for challenge, increased responsibility, achievement, professional and personal growth, compensation for your effort, etc. Your answer should convey that you have done extensive research and discovered that the job of pharmaceutical sales is the ideal fit for you. For example, "Though there are many aspects of my current position that I enjoy, I have found that my skills and abilities are best suited to pharmaceutical sales. I desire the challenge for professional and personal growth within the industry and particularly with XYZ Pharmaceuticals."

72) Are you still employed at the last organization listed on your resume?

This is easy if the answer is, "Yes." If not, answer the question honestly, with confidence and in a matter-of-fact tone. Today's economy has brought about many job changes. Being "between jobs" does not carry the stigma it once did now that we operate in a constantly changing business environment. An example of an answer could be, "I was one of nine individuals not retained with the organization. Our profits did not meet expectations. There were many cutbacks within all departments. Due to my tenure, I was not retained." Then stop and allow the interview to move forward from there.

73) Will you have a tough time becoming acquainted with a new industry after being with the same organization for awhile?

Example answer: "Not at all. I have worked for several different managers and interacted with numerous departments during my time with ABC Incorporated. I am very flexible and learn quickly. I know I can contribute to your sales team from the start."

74) You have had numerous positions over the past four years. How do I know that you will stay at XYZ Pharmaceutical Company?

Job changes are always good if they involve and increase in challenge, responsibility, or compensation. Show the benefit and progress of your career moves. Some factors may have been out of your control. Examples are acquisitions, mergers, layoffs, relocation, etc. Be confident, direct, and honest in your reply. For example: "With each new position, I have progressed in achieving my career goals. Over the past several months, I have redefined these goals due to extensive research, networking, completing a pharmaceutical preceptorship, etc. I know that pharmaceutical sales is exactly where I want to achieve those goals and XYZ Pharmaceutical Company is the company in which I will excel."

75) How long have you been looking for a pharmaceutical sales position?

Here is an opportunity for you to describe your research and extensive knowledge of this industry. If you are interviewing with another pharmaceutical company, disclose where you are in the interview process (second, third, final interview, or offer stage). This response will evoke the competitive nature in the interviewer. Keep the time you have been looking as short as possible because managers may feel that you may have been passed over for a particular reason.

76) Why haven't you secured an offer to date?

This is a hardball question. It is meant to see if you can be thrown off your game. There is no right or wrong answer. Remain confident. Display your knowledge of the industry and companies with whom you have interviewed. Include offers if you have had any. For example, "I have had an offer with ABC Pharma, but the geography and the timing were not right for me. The position you have available is perfect, and I am ready to make a commitment to your organization."

77) How did you do on your last performance review? What strengths and areas of improvement did you manager observe?

This is a repeat of "tell me your weaknesses." Choose and explain the steps you took to improve yourself. Examples may be that you are impatient with the others in your department, or you tend to take on too much. You have remedied this by gaining a better understanding of other people's work habits, developing time lines and new tactics of time management.

78) Tell me about the best manager you have ever had?

This is time to give the most praise, because a hiring manager wants to see that you can interact well with management. Explain your position, how you followed your manager's direction, how management monitored your progress, and gave the appropriate praise and comments.

79) Tell me about the worst manager you have ever had?

Using the same strategies in discussing your weaknesses, avoid stating that you have ever had a bad manager. "I have learned from all of the managers I have had in my professional career. If I had to pick a particular competency in a manager that could have been demonstrated better, it may have been enthusiasm and keeping our team motivated."

80) Describe in one word what selling means to you.

Many different words can be used, but stick to the request for one word. Suggestions are value, satisfaction, integrity, relationship, or success.

81) How is your driving record?

This question is a practical matter for the company to determine eligibility for hire. It is usually asked in the screening interview and is a question on the employment application. Your driving record will always be part of the background checks. Some companies will run the background check before making an offer, while others will make the offer first, contingent on the background checks. Since driving is a requirement on the job, and you will drive a company car, the insurance requirements demand that you have a good record. Moving violations are usually no problem unless you have a license suspension or revocation on your record. However, DWI and DUI in the past three to four years will eliminate you from consideration for most companies. The best way to answer this question is to know what is and is not on your record. Include in your answer only felony or misdemeanor convictions, which is normally all that is requested. Citations such as moving violations can also be requested. If you do not know what your record shows and you suspect there may be something there, find out. Know what your record states and the state's laws in terms of how long infractions are maintained on your record, and always be straightforward. When necessary, admit your mistake, what you have learned from it, and that your record since then has been impeccable.

82) Your product and price is the same as a competitor's. How would you sell your product?

This is when it comes down to relationships. People buying from people applies in pharmaceuticals just as any other sales venture. Give examples of how you develop rapport, provide excellent service, follow-up, call frequency to establish physician habits, the value you add, and that you close for the business. Often, this business goes to the sales representative who both earns the right to ask for it and asks for it.

83) A doctor says that she is going to stop writing prescriptions for your drug and is switching to the competition. What do you do?

This question, like many of this type, is looking for your selling skills. While this is at first a bad situation to encounter with a customer there is a positive aspect. Because the physician bothered to let you know she is switching products, it indicates a trusting relationship and is an invitation to talk about it. The doctor has probably heard something negative about your product, and now needs reassurance to rebuild confidence in you and your product. You will no doubt have a detailed discussion beginning with asking all the questions and listening well. Collect all the concerns, objections and misunderstandings the doctor may have before going off on a tangent. Use your best listening and probing skills with non-defensive posture and verbal tone. Once you have all the information, you can address it.

84) What do you expect is the most difficult or challenging part of being a Pharmaceutical Rep?

This question is seeking your understanding of the job and whether you believe you have the skills and confidence to be successful. There is no right or wrong answer here, but "physician access" or "time with the physician" is a solid answer. Do not wait for the next question, "What would you do about it?" Answer that question at the same time.

85) What would you do to gain access to and spend more time with doctors?

This will be a common question since it is the biggest challenge you will face. Practice your answers before you interview. Some of the obvious responses are:

• Contacting the doctor at hospital displays.
• Invite him to educational programs.
• Discover how they spend their free time.
• Offer to entertain the doctor and a spouse or guest.
• Always provide new information and value on your calls.
• Have other "hard-to-see" doctors give you a recommendation.
• Call on the doctor with increased frequency to better your chances of getting in.
• Develop rapport with the staff and make a "friend" who will give you the inside track.
• Acknowledge this is a challenge to be met with creativity, persistence, and patience.

There are no "magic answers," every doctor is different. State that you would take a long-term view of this situation to develop a specific plan of action for the less available physicians in your territory. You know that even doctors with a "no see" policy will see certain sales representatives who offer them value, and whom they respect. You may consider writing to the doctor and asking for a one-time meeting that will take no more than five minutes of their time. Promise that if you do not provide value to his expectations you will not ask him again. When you do get access, request permission for the next meeting before you leave. Finally, know that your relationship skills are critical and you must show genuine concern and interest in the physician. Show confidence and believe in your ability to influence that customer.

86) A doctor is resistant to trying your product. What would you do?

Physicians "buy" like any other group of individuals. Some will respond quickly and try whatever is new. These "early adopters" are mostly focused on effectiveness of the product. Others are cautious and wait for information from those who did try it first. These "late adopters" are more focused on safety (side effects). The majority of physicians are in between these two extremes. Once you know you are dealing with a late adopter, you can approach him or her accordingly. In addition to rapport building, probing, and the listening skills that you would always use, this doctor may respond if you narrow the product to a specific patient type. Gain commitment for that patient only. Discover which doctors he associates with, either professionally or personally, who prescribes your product. Knowing that other doctors prescribe your product may give him the confidence he needs to try it.

87) Your counterpart is having problems with his day-to-day responsibilities. His sales results are showing it and affecting your share as well. What do you do?

If you are an experienced sales representative, you should offer your assistance in a positive manner. Maybe something you know, or a way you approach your position, can help this individual. This shows your competencies around "teamwork." If this has failed and you feel that the individual is harming your district sales, then it is a concern that you will want to address with your manager in an appropriate manner.

88) You have spent all of your month's expenses on a luncheon with three doctors and their staff. Just before the lunch, one of the staff members says that two of the doctors will not be there. What do you do?

You have to be flexible and creative in this situation. Obviously, you are going to follow-through on your commitment. On the bright side, you will have more time with the doctor who is there. Next, you can leverage the situation with that doctor and the staff by asking what they would suggest could be done about meeting with those who did not join your group. Never simply excuse it. Create urgency or mild tension by reacting in a serious manner. Let them know you are out on a limb financially to provide this lunch. This will put them in the position of trying to help you out. They may offer to schedule appointments with the missing doctors to make up for it. If not, ask for an appointment or another way of accessing those doctors when they return.

89) Why should I hire you?

This is a typical "tough" question, but it is a great opportunity when you get it. Being prepared with more information will help you answer this by asking for the job. By this point in the interview, you may have already asked the manager what he or she is looking for in an ideal candidate. If not, this is the time to ask. You will show confidence in your demeanor by looking right back at the interviewer and asking, "To help me focus my answer, what are you looking for in the ideal candidate?" Then tailor your full response to his or her "hot buttons." In general, you will hit the core competencies for the job. For example, "I have demonstrated the drive to achieve (as evidenced by previous sales success); I have shown you that I am creative, persistent, self-motivated, and a fast learner. I have thoroughly researched the industry and this company and know what the position requires. I am excited about the challenges ahead and am confident that I will be a successful member of your team. I want the job! Is there anything else you need to know in order to make me the offer? Great!"

90) Describe yourself in one word.

This question is not as important as it sounds. The intention is to see how you think on your feet. As long as you maintain composure and deliver a one-word answer, you have succeeded. Keep a word in mind so you can deliver it without hesitation. Pick something you can back up with specific examples of when you demonstrated that aspect or behavior. Here are some ideas:

Creative	Persistent	Consistent
Sincere	Determined	Competitive
Motivated		

91) Since you do not have sales experience what makes you believe you will be successful in pharmaceutical sales?

The only indicator of future success is past performance. You will make the case for success in sales by demonstrating that you have succeeded in every professional and personal endeavor. You have developed the competencies for success in other areas and will do the same for sales.

PROFESSIONAL ATTIRE

Your efforts in networking, research, and resumes have met with success. You have just been called for an initial interview with the District Manager of XYZ Pharmaceutical Company. It is time to get dressed. You scrutinize your wardrobe for the perfect look, one that says, "I am the qualified individual for this position." Why are your attire and appearance more important than your attributes, skills, and abilities? Because there is that one hurdle that you must cross with every new encounter—the critical first impression.

Sociologists use the term "halo effect" to describe the first 30 seconds of a meeting. In those first 30 seconds, people generally make up their minds about you. They decide whether they have just met someone who is competent, genuine, and "on top of it" or not. Your dress is a nonverbal communication as to what you think about yourself, your attitude toward business, your goals, and how well you regard the other individuals with whom you are meeting. Right or wrong, decisions about your ability and character are based upon the interviewer's response to your appearance. It is assumed that anyone who can handle personal details well will be just as meticulous with the details of the job. Thus, your goal is to create the halo effect for yourself. Professional attire, an engaging manner, a firm handshake, and an air of energy and vitality will set the stage on which you will perform to your highest level.

Beyond first impressions, the way you dress indicates your sense of professional judgment and establishes your credibility. While you are selling yourself orally during your interview nonverbal communication, including attire will either reinforce what you are saying or undermine your own words.

Recent college graduates may not yet own expensive business attire. Shop for deals on wool fabric suits, but spend the extra money to get it tailored to fit correctly. You can get away with a lesser quality suit by wearing higher quality accessories, such as shoes and ties. The hiring process for pharmaceutical sales may require two or three interviews. Be prepared with two interview suits, if possible. If not, accessorize with ties, shirt styles (men keep it all white), and shoes for a slightly different look. Finally, make sure your suit is clean and freshly pressed.

Putting time, energy, and expense into your professional appearance will always pay you back. Think of it as an investment in yourself and your career. You will command authority and assume credibility beyond that which you currently possess. "Looking the part" is critical during the interview process. The interviewer will begin to visualize you in the job instead of just another interviewing candidate. Never underestimate the power of the first impression. Meticulous attention to your appearance will put you at an advantage.

The following are guidelines for women followed by those for men.

WOMEN'S GUIDELINES FOR INTERVIEWING DRESS

- No outfit is more effective for an interview than the matched suited skirt. Research has shown the most successful colors are black, navy, and gray, and you should pair it with a high-necked white or ivory silk blouse. Pantyhose should always be lighter in color of your clothing. A medium-healed pump is safest. Shoes should be well polished, clean, and darker than the suit.
- Practicality dictates that a woman may carry a purse as well as a briefcase. You must manage both comfortably when shaking hands, sitting down, etc. A briefcase only is quite acceptable, as is a nice leather portfolio. A leather portfolio is good for note taking during the inter view, but a new legal pad will do just fine. You will need a briefcase for your interviewing files and materials, and it should be leather and the best you can afford. Avoid company names or logos on your accessories.
- Your hair should be neat and off the shoulders in a manageable style. Avoid bows and compli cated styles. Your hair should draw attention to and complement you face.

- A touch of makeup is appropriate. Light makeup will enhance a woman's professional image. The goal is to wear makeup without looking made up.
- Nails should be short and rounded. The only appropriate nail colors are clear or natural; a French manicure is also acceptable and distinctive.
- Jewelry should be simple and professional; avoid anything that will draw attention away from you. Gold or silver chains are smart. If worn, lapel pins should be elegant. Earrings lend authority and professionalism, and should be small and simple, no bigger than a quarter. Dangles or hoops are inappropriate.
- Wear a nice analog style watch (not digital) because analog watches project more of a tradi tional/formal business appearance versus a sports/digital watch; a wedding ring, if married, with or without the engagement ring. No other rings.
- Use a fine gold or sterling pen.
- There should be no perfume or fragrance. Many individuals have chemical sensitivities that can be aggravated by hair spray or perfume.

MEN'S GUIDELINES FOR INTERVIEWING DRESS

- The two-piece wool business single-breasted suit is the foundation. Research shows that the most authoritative colors are dark blue and dark gray. These two colors look good on everyone. Use a traditional, conservative style versus a European designer one. The fit is more important than the quality of the wool, so spend your money on the tailoring. Button the top button while standing or walking, unbutton it when sitting. Pocket flaps should be worn out of the pockets.
- Shirts should be solid white and all cotton for interviews. Use a straight collar instead of a button-down collar for the conservative, slightly more formal look. Avoid collars with snaps or ones that require collar pins. Your shirt should be professionally laundered, and starched for a crisp look. Pens go in the coat pocket, not the shirt pocket.
- Wear a new, fashionable conservative silk tie. Choose a solid colored tie that complements, not matches, your suit. Good colors are maroon, crimson, or navy blue (except with a navy blue suit). Patterned ties such as stripes, foulards, or small dots are acceptable. Avoid paisleys, prints, club ties, insignias, or depiction of any identifiable cartoon, or other characters. Skip the pocket-hand kerchief. The bottom point of the tie should line up with the middle of the belt buckle. Do not wear a tie clasp or a pin of any kind.
- Avoid wearing an overcoat; it is cumbersome to handle.
- Avoid monogrammed belt buckles, or designer initials and monograms anywhere. A plain black leather belt will complement the navy or gray suit.
- Shoes should be good quality and newly polished. A laced, plain-toe or wing-tipped oxford is best. Tasseled loafers can project casualness. Err on the conservative side. Black and cordovan are appropriate colors. Socks should be over-the-calf or long enough to cover your legs when sitting or if your pant-leg rides up. Do not cross your legs during an interview. Use a solid colored sock in black for black shoes and in navy for cordovan shoes. In some areas of the United States, cowboy boots are not out of place for business wear, but are best avoided for interviewing.
- Hair should be short and neat. Beards and mustaches are a means of self-expression and identity. However, for the most professional look, be clean-shaven during your job search. You can always grow it back later.
- Wear a nice analog (not digital) wristwatch. Do not wear rubber sport watches. The only ring should be a wedding band, if married. Avoid other rings, bracelets, lapel pins, or other jewelry. Cuff links are fine if they are simple, plain gold. Use a pen of excellent quality and keep it handy in your coat pocket.

- Your briefcase should be professional, leather, well polished, and dark colored. A leather portfolio is especially valuable for taking notes during the interview. You will need a briefcase for the interviewing files and materials you have collected. Avoid company names or logos on your accessories.
- Men's fingernails should be short and rounded, clean and buffed to a shine. Trim and clean the cuticles for a detail-oriented look.
- There should be no cologne; avoid anything with a fragrance. Chemical sensitivities apply to many people.

[SAMPLE LETTER: INTERVIEW FOLLOW-UP]

October 26, 2001

Janet Lynn Jones
1234 West Drive
Salestown, USA

Joe Interviewer
XYZ Pharmaceutical Corp
1234 South Drive
Drugtown, USA

Dear Mr. Interviewer:

Thank you for the opportunity to discuss the Sales Representative position with XYZ Pharmaceuticals. It was a pleasure meeting with you today.

I am excited about our conversation and am especially impressed with the autonomy given to each sales representative and the challenge that it offers. You are looking for a determined self-starter with a successful sales background. I am looking for a company that rewards individual effort.

A career in pharmaceutical sales at XYZ is an excellent match for my skills and career objectives. I really want this position, for I know that I can make a significant contribution to your team.

Thank you again for you time and consideration. I look forward to hearing from you soon.

Sincerely,

Janet Lynn Jones

Chapter 7

Your Questions

This chapter provides you with ammunition and questions you should ask during the various stages of the interviewing process. Why should you be asking questions? The point to having your own questions to ask is twofold. First, you will demonstrate your preparation, awareness of the position, and communication skills. Second, you need to evaluate the person and company that you are considering joining, perhaps for your entire career.

There are two main questions. (1) Is the organization the best for you? (2) Can you work with, or for, this individual? You must answer each other's questions during the interview process to move forward and result in your employment.

This chapter offers twenty-five questions that are appropriate for you to ask the interviewer. Pharmaceuticalsales.com has listed the questions in the chronological order of the interview process. Avoid asking the more advanced questions too early, but use your discretion. Change the style to match your own, and have fun with it!

Many of these questions are similar to those you may have already asked in your networking. If you are already aware of information from your pharmaceuticalsales.com networking phase, interlace it into your interview process. As discussed in Chapters 4 and 5, presenting your knowledge about the company demonstrates preparedness and drive. For example, instead of asking the District Manager, "How many territories are in your district," use that piece of information as a lead-in to another question: "I understand there are twelve territories in your district (information from your networking). How does the open territory's performance compare with the other territories in the district?"

TIP: *Every interviewer usually concludes by saying, "Do you have any questions for me?" Prepare five to ten important questions that you want answered. It is completely acceptable to refer to your notes during the interview.*

SCREENING AND INITIAL INTERVIEWS

1. How did this position become available with your company?

The answer could be that it was opened due a promotion, transfer, expansion, or termination.

2. What qualifications and qualities are you looking for in the ideal candidate?

This is a critical question. It uncovers the manager's "hot buttons," or the key characteristics in a job candidate. Ask this at the start of, or early in, the interview. The answer is significant, and should guide you as you match your own qualifications and qualities to those the manager is looking for. Emphasize your attributes that respond to the stated requirements.

3. I have completed many hours of research on a career in the pharmaceutical sales industry and your company. I am extremely interested in this position. When can we meet to discuss it in detail?

This is a solid close for the initial interview process. Be sure to mail a follow-up letter within 24 hours.

TIP: *Often, initial screening interviews are accomplished over the telephone. Be free of interrup-tions. Turn off call waiting by pressing 70 before the scheduled interview time. Have all infor-mation, notes, and questions in front of you.*

4. What is the geography of this territory?

Examples may be rural or metropolitan, certain cities, towns, or zip codes. The interviewer's answer may give you an opportunity to state that you are familiar with some of the various areas. Example: I attended school in Bryn Mawr, PA., and am very familiar with the area.

5. What are the major accounts in this territory? Who are the essential customers?

This answer will tell you who brings in the most business in the district. Possibilities may include an individual or a group of specialists who are considered to be "thought leaders." These are the experts in a given specialty, and are highly respected by other physicians in the area. Their importance is due to this significant influence. Pharmaceutical companies assign responsibility for calling on these thought leaders to their best and most experienced representatives. Other examples could be a large uni-versity-based teaching institution that has an influence in the area, or perhaps a large retail pharmacy chain that is dominant in the district.

TIP: *One purpose of asking questions is to gain information. Another reason is to discover what is important to the interviewer. When you uncover something of significance in your interveiw with the District Manager, refer to that item in your follow-up letter. This demonstrates that you listen and comprehend what is important to your customer.*

6. What type of physician specialties is your main target audience?

Examples: family practice, internal medicine, surgery, pediatrics, dermatology, psychiatry, aller-gy and immunology, rheumatology, obstetrics, oncology, and urology. A growing number of physicians concentrate their practices on pain management as well.

7. How many territories and representatives are there in this district?

Districts may average seven to twelve representatives. Regions may have five to seven districts. This is information you may already have from your networking contacts with a representative from this company.

8. What are the various divisions of the sales force?

Different pharmaceutical companies are similar in some ways and vary greatly in others. One area where they differ is in the structure of the sales force and the various divisions or groups within it. This answer gives you the sales specialties and challenging directions in which your career could go. Examples include a Hospital Sales Force, Diabetes Specialists, National Account Team, Managed Care Account Representatives, Governmental Affairs, and many others.

9. How is this territory performing to budget? How does it rank in the district?

You need to know the current state of the business in what may be your new territory. Is the ter-ritory operating at 10% below budget or 20% over budget. Whatever the answer, your goal is to improve upon it.

10. What is the total sales revenue of this territory? How many prescriptions are being written in this territory?

With this question, you are asking how many dollars worth of sales you will be responsible for when you take over the territory. The quantity of prescriptions is also significant because your goal will be to increase both dollar sales and prescription volume.

11. Describe the training program for new representatives to continue education and development programs.

You want to choose a company that is committed to training and development. You realize the importance that skills and education are to your success and career advancement. This question will communicate your desire for a continuous educational cycle throughout your career.

12. Are there any products that have been submitted to the Food and Drug Administration (FDA) for marketing approval or which are in Phase III of development?

From your research, you may already know the answer to this question, however, asking shows that you are seeking information on the company's future over the next several years. You want to choose a company that has a full pipeline of new products in the near future. It means the company is more stable and can withstand competition from other brand name and generic manufacturers. If a product has been submitted to the FDA, it is close to approval and may be launched to the market soon. If a product is in Phase III of development it is in final stages of human research and may soon be submitted to the FDA for the approval process. The FDA approval takes one to two years.

13. What products are in early stages of development (Phase I and Phase II)?

This answer provides you with a longer-term picture of the company's future. Phases I and II are conducted in the initial R&D process for newly discovered compounds. Phase I is conducted in the laboratory and in animals. Phase II begins small-scale safety testing on humans. District managers may not be aware of products in early development.

14. Which therapeutic areas or specific diseases does the company target for new product development?

Companies will specialize, much as physicians do, by concentrating their R&D efforts on a limited number of diseases. Are the targeted therapeutic areas (such as cardiac diseases, depression, or diabetes) similar to current treatments, or is the company expanding its research into other possible solutions? Do they have a focus for research? Does it match their product line. This question will uncover the general direction, or strategy of the organization.

15. Does the company co-market with another pharmaceutical company?

Co-marketing (also called co-promoting) is an agreement between two companies to promote the same product at the same time. Co-marketing usually involves a trade-off in which each company takes on one of the other company's products, though not necessarily at the same time. Example: XYZ Pharmaceutical Company is co-marketing a new antibiotic from Widget Pharmacal. Next year when XYZ Pharmaceutical company introduces their new diabetes agent, Widget Pharmacal will co-promote it in return. This question can give you insight into how aggressive the company is in hitting the bottom line. Are they willing to use co-marketing arrangements to meet sales and profit objectives?

16. I like what I have learned about the company, and I have demonstrated that I can contribute and will add value. I want this position. What is our next step in the process?

This is a good closing question to get yourself to the next interview, but it is aggressive and should be used at or near the end. This helps you assess the interviewer's interest in you and moves you forward in the process. Be firm and convincing. Watch for the manager's reactions.

TIP: *Always use a strong close at or near the end of each interview. It gives the interviewer confidence that you will close in a sales call, too. It will also give you immediate responses as to how you rate with the interviewer. When you close, use a question like the one above, accompanied by a confident statement that you WANT THE JOB.*

Second and/or Final Interviews

The following questions are appropriate for more advanced, or second and third interviews. You are now a serious contender for the offer, and you should ask more in depth questions. These hit harder and are designed to give you the information you need to make the best decision when you receive an offer. You need to know where you are in the interviewing process and what is still ahead of you. Alternatively, how many interviews does it generally take to get the job? This information helps you plan and enact your strategy.

17. May I contact the previous Pharmaceutical Sales Representative that occupied this territory

This is a risky question. Ask why the territory is open before asking to contact the previous representative. If the territory is open due to a termination, do not bother asking if you can contact him or her. If the previous representative was promoted within the company, the district manager would probably welcome you to contact him or her. If the previous representative left the company voluntarily, the district manager could answer either way. Regardless of the answer, it is a smart question to ask and shows you are thorough about your research. You take seriously your decision to join a company with which you plan to spend a long career.

18. May I contact any representatives that report to you?

As in the previous question, you want to gain more understanding about this company and your decision to work for it. You need to be confident that this is the one for you. Contacting other representatives is a good way to gain this insight. Ask them why they work for the company, what their level of satisfaction is, and what their goals are (see networking questions in Chapter 5 for more ideas). In addition, by asking this question you will gauge the manager's self-assurance in his or her managerial style. Ask yourself if this is the right person to help you achieve a successful career.

TIP: *Be sure you know as much about a company as you can before joining it. Always speak to the previous representative (as discussed in question 17) and at least one representative that currently reports to the district manager who would be hiring you. Do this before accepting a position with any organization.*

19. How would you describe your management style and that of the company?

This is an invitation for the interviewer to speak. Listen as the manager describes his or her own style and management philosophy within the organization. Is this is a good fit for you?

20. How does the company measure sales representatives' performance? How is it rewarded? What percentage of total compensation is base salary versus bonus?

This answer should provide insight into the sales tracking mechanism that is used (see Chapter 2 for more discussion of sales tracking). You will also hear about the commission plans, bonus structure, field promotions, merchandise awards, and incentive trips. You want to discover how much of your total compensation is at risk depending on sales performance. Remember that your compensation is mostly a fixed base salary.

21. How long do you believe it would take your new Sales Representative to generate significant results in the territory?

This answer tells you how quickly the manager expects to see results, and how he perceives the learning curve.

22. How do you evaluate your sales representative and how often?

This question offers insight into the manager's style of presenting feedback. Good managers will give frequent and consistent criticism or advice in addition to routine performance reviews, which are either semiannual or annual. You need to know what to expect in terms of suggestions and recommendations.

23. With excellent performance, how long should a new Sales Representative expect to gain experience in his or her territory before being eligible for promotion?

You will communicate a desire to climb the corporate ladder with this question. If you do not have that desire at this point, that is fine, but it opens the door for the manager to relay some career success stories of individuals or themselves within the organization. The answer tells you what you can expect for you or other representatives.

24. Describe the typical career path for your Sales Representatives.

The key to this question, as opposed to the previous one, is that you are asking about the potential advancement for the person who stays in sales throughout his or her career. As discussed in Chapter 2, field sales are a career that is challenging and rewarding. There are many opportunities for promotions and advancement other than entering sales management or a home office position. This answer will vary. You may hear about increasing levels of recognition, salary, prestigious titles, and additional district, regional, or national responsibilities.

25. Considering what I have learned in our interview process, plus my research and networking within the industry, I know I can make a strong contribution to your district and your organization. I want this position. May I do the job for you?

This is your final statement. The wording should match your style, but deliver it emphatically. The purpose of the close is twofold. First, you need to clearly communicate that you want the job. Second, you want to uncover any lingering objections or questions the interviewer may have. This may be your last chance to make your case. Although it has been known to happen, you will probably not get an offer or rejection on the spot. However, you should get some valuable comments. You will most likely receive a "qualified" maybe, pending an interview with another final candidate, reference checks, or simply the need for further consideration.

TIP: *When you touch the door knob or cross the threshold to exit the room, turn back to the interviewer and state it one more time: "Thank you for your time. I want to do the job for you." Use your own words, but say it with conviction!*

Chapter 8

Decisions, Decisions

Congratulations! You have just completed your interviewing process. You have networked, researched, studied, prepared, interviewed, and followed-up with a letter. Only few things can happen next: you will receive an offer, be turned down, or asked to return for another interview.

As you await the District Manager's decision, you will probably be contemplating the following thoughts: What will s/he say? How should you respond? What will you do if the answer is no? What if you get the offer but do not want the job? What if you want a better starting salary? As these questions suggest, there is still plenty of work ahead for you no matter what the decision.

THE REJECTION

First, let us examine the bad news—you are turned down for the position. It is important to remember that it is not the end of the world; it happens to everyone. If you respond to this unfortunate situation correctly, it will turn out to be a positive experience for your career.

How should you reply? It is natural to be disappointed. However, it will serve you well to remain positive and courteous. Continue the same professionalism and determination that got you to the interview in the first place. Be persistent with the interviewer until you get direct comments about your interview. Find out what you can do to improve your qualifications or interviewing techniques in the future. Ask the interviewer for honest advice. Ask for one or two key strengths that he or she feels you possess. What are essential areas in which you could improve and how? In other words, accept the opinion from a manager who has spent time getting to know you. If it is honest advice, it will be valuable for you.

Usually, the position will already have been offered and accepted before the runners-up are contacted. However, it can happen that a candidate receives multiple offers, accepting employment with one company and then, within weeks or months, accepting another. Thus, the same position may be open again. Alternatively, a different territory in the same district could become available, and since you have already been through the interview process, you can state your interest. Therefore, it is important to keep the door open for yourself. Tell the interviewer that you still want the job, and if their top-choice candidate does not work out, you are willing to make a commitment. Communicate that if any other sales territory becomes available, you would like to be considered for that job as well. The benefit to the manager is that he or she will not have to go through the entire hiring process all over again if they can call you and make an immediate offer.

TIP: *Tell the Manager that you will call back in three months to check for any potential new open ings. Be sure to schedule it on your calendar and make the call regardless of your job situation at that time. If you already have an offer or are working with another company, explain that you just wanted to follow-up on your commitment.*

Even a rejection should be followed with a letter of appreciation to the interviewer. An example of a letter you might use for this purpose is at the end of this chapter.

THE OFFER

Next, the good news! You have an offer for the position you want. Congratulations! Now you are ready to accept, decline, or negotiate.

Regardless of your intention, pharmaceuticalsales.com suggests that you not respond immediately with your decision. You have worked long and hard for this offer and your work has been rewarded. Take some time to think about it. You need at least twenty-four hours to consider it, sleep on it, and discuss it with your spouse or significant other. The company has kept you waiting. It is acceptable to ask for as much time as you need to make your decision.

It is also important to request a letter of the job offer. This letter describes everything that the organization is proposing to you. You can review it and make sure that no misunderstandings exist before you make your decision. This strategy gives you time to think about the details of the offer and review other offers you may have. You will also demonstrate to your potential new employer that you are mature and serious about your decision. Furthermore, you have been patiently waiting for the decision from them. They will understand giving you time to make a thoughtful decision—and will appreciate your request.

If the offer meets your requirements and you want the job, accept it. If you would like more money, take this opportunity to ask for it. For example, "I am looking for a base salary of $35,000. What flexibility do you have in your offer?" If you are struggling with whether to ask for more, some quick calculations may motivate you. Consider that even a modest increase ($500 to $1000) in your starting salary accumulates from year to year. Over a 20 year career, compounded annually, this could easily add up to over $25,000. Because all future increases are based on a percentage of your current salary, all your subsequent raises will be larger. In addition to the financial motive, negotiating for more money demonstrates your desire to achieve more—an excellent trait for a sales person. This also builds your negotiating skills. Try it!

You are all set with your start date, yet there are more questions. Should you suspend your job search immediately? The logical response is yes, however, the consensus at pharmaceuticalsales.com is that such a decision may be premature.

Consider this scenario: You are excited about accepting the offer and want to get underway with your new job. During your job search, you have followed the strategy outlined in Insight. All of your efforts with other companies are still paying dividends. Ironically, the week after you accept your offer, a company with which you previously interviewed calls because of an unforeseen vacancy. The vacancy is actually a better fit for your interests and the complete package is significantly more attractive. This situation is quite common. In your excitement over your new position you think that it would be unethical to continue the interview process, and politely inform the company who called that you are not interested. Unfortunately, two months later you and your new manager are not quite satisfied and numerous disappointments with the new organization have made themselves apparent.

Because of scenarios such as this one, we urge you to keep your options open as much as possible. It is not disloyal to leave a job in which there is no mutual benefit. Over time, it may be worse to stay in a job where you are not 100% committed. Integrity and professionalism are always paramount and lead to a more satisfying career. Be sure that you do not alienate yourself from the organization, sales managers, or human resources executives that you may want to work with in the future. A word to the wise: The old adage, "It's a small world," applies to the entire pharmaceutical industry.

TIP: *Consider all options with professionalism and courtesy. You will always benefit.*

Finally, the remaining possible outcome is that the decision has not been reached and more time is needed. This may occur for several reasons. First, the company may have decided not to fill the position after all. In an ever-changing and complex business environment, such as the pharmaceutical industry, this may occur when a company is in a state of flux due to a merger, product sell-off, acquisition, or a change in corporate strategy or direction. Another reason for a delay may be that the District Manager and Regional Manager are not completely satisfied that they have considered all the qualified candidates. They are still searching. If this is the case, you will probably not be told that you are still considered a viable candidate.

Finally, they may simply want to bring you back for another interview. There may be someone else in the organization for you to meet before making the final decision. The purpose of this may be to get another person's perception about you and whether that person agrees that you are a fit for the company.

Regardless of the reason for a delay, your strategy should remain the same. Continue to be upbeat, positive, and emphatic about your desire and commitment to the position and the company. Do whatever it takes in terms of additional interviews or company contacts. Follow each contact or telephone call with a brief note. Offer to call every week or so for updates on the process. Thorough communication will demonstrate your commitment and sales abilities. The manager is also interested in keeping you interested during the period of delay. A good manager knows keeping you excited and positive about the job until a final decision has been fully implemented benefits their corporation. The manager wants you to know that you are his or her number one choice. This is motivating for you and helps keep any candidate's energy level high.

[SAMPLE LETTER: FOLLOW-UP TO 'REJECTION']

August 4, 2001

Janet Lynn Jones
631 Any Street
Anytown, USA 54321

Bill Franklin
District Manager
XYZ Pharmaceutical Company
12345 East Drive Way
Newark, New Jersey 01234

Dear Mr. Franklin,

Again, thank you for the opportunity to interview with you and XYZ Pharmaceutical Company. I know that I can make a significant contribution to your team.

If a position becomes available in the near future, please contact me. My home telephone is 555-5555. As we agreed, I will contact you in three months to discuss future opportunities.

Sincerely,

Janet M. Jones

Conclusion

Your Commitment

Anne Clayton wrote and published *Insight* with the confidence that it would empower you to fulfill your goal of breaking into a rewarding career in pharmaceutical sales. As you follow the strategy that you have just read about, Anne would like you to keep in mind these words of encouragement:

- It is common to receive rejections during your networking and interviewing process.
- Remember that everyone will experience the same rate of rejection.
- Not everyone will be as determined in meeting his or her own goals.
- Be persistent and resolute; set yourself apart from those who will become discouraged or quit after one or two sessions of interviews.

You are learning and applying a process or method. These skills are valuable to you regardless of the outcome of each individual contact or interview. Your experience with this challenging process helps you grow and become better with every effort you make. Thus, as in all sales professions, even in rejection there is progress and advancement toward your goals.

Once you have reached your goal, live up to your promises to the interviewer and the company. Continue to apply the diligence and determination you showed during your job search. After you have accepted the offer, continue to differentiate yourself from the other candidates your company has hired who may be your new co-workers and peers. You have set a high standard for yourself throughout the interviewing and candidate selection process that will now provide momentum for your success throughout your career.

Upon accepting the offer, begin by sending brief letters to your new manager and any other managers, directors, and human resources personnel with whom you had contact during the hiring process. State that you are excited to be aboard and looking forward to meeting your professional career goals and the business goals of your new company.

Apply yourself diligently during the various training programs in which you will participate. Professionalism at all times is the rule. Bear in mind that the quality of your performance is always important, and you must continue to make your mark by excelling in your initial training.

Continue your research and networking; these skills will always enhance your career. However, focus on getting to know the sales representatives, managers, companies, and products in and around your territory, rather than uncovering job prospects. You will encounter many opportunities to meet other sales representatives as you move about in doctor's offices, hospitals, clinics, conventions, meetings, and seminars. Use these occasions to introduce yourself and learn more about your new colleagues. Ascertain what they are doing that can be helpful to you. Talk about your work habits and practices, not about your sales messages and strategies on your particular products.

Do representatives from other companies seem satisfied with their organizations, or do they complain about their work, their managers, or their products? This information provides insight that can be used to promote your product over a competitor's, or find possible job candidates for your own company. Frequently, you may receive financial gains for your referrals.

As you have learned in your research and networking process, some metropolitan areas have professional associations for pharmaceutical representatives. Find out if one exists in your area and check into it. Joining a professional organization opens new doors and enhances your own career as people learn who you are.

You have learned valuable skills that will be practical throughout your career. Work hard, be your best, and always differentiate yourself from your competition and your peers.
Best of success!

APPENDIX

Company Profiles

The following company profiles and worksheets will complement your research efforts. Building your own files on these organizations will provide keys to success in the future; add to this overview information. These worksheets are located at the end of the Appendix and should be used to record your notes and organize your information on a specific company. Set up a profile worksheet for every company you research or interact with. Make copies of blank worksheets as needed. Update your files as you complete your research and uncover vital information from your networking contacts.

When you have an interview coming up, study all the information you have gathered. Make sure it is up to date regarding any new products or company news. Yes, you will find new information. Review annual reports, newspapers, web sites and networking with representatives, and document your research. Use the research and networking resources from Chapter 4 and Chapter 5. Practice incorporating what you know into your interviewing approach, as discussed in Chapter 6 and Chapter 7.

You will also find a list of names, addresses and contact information on the top contract sales organizations. There are great opportunities with these companies. As contract sales forces become more accepted and popular among manufacturers they are frequently expanding and hiring sales representatives.

There are many other pharmaceutical companies than pharmaceuticalsales.com has provided in the following company profiles. Thus, you should complete your own profile on each company you contact. Do your own research. Always be prepared with any organization. You will achieve your career goal if you follow the strategy and if you are persistent. Work hard, be patient, and strive for the best!

Please note—pharmaceuticalsales.com does not offer opinions, rankings or endorsements of any specific pharmaceutical company.

ABBOTT LABORATORIES
100 ABBOTT PARK ROAD
ABBOTT PARK, IL. 60064
847.937.6100
NYSE: ABT
ABBOTT. COM
ROSS.COM

Summary: Abbott Laboratories is a global company producing medications, nutritional supplements, and products used in hospitals and laboratories. The pharmaceutical division develops antibiotic, anti-infective, antihypertensive, oncology, thyroid, and other medications. Ross Products, a division of Abbott produces nutritional products and pharmaceuticals. Tap Pharmaceutical Products Inc. is Abbott's joint venture with Takeda Chemical Industries Ltd.

History: Wallace Abbott a medical doctor established the Abbott Alkaloidal Company in a Chicago in 1888 to sell his formulations. The company went public in 1929 and by the mid 1930's opened branches in South America, Mexico and Britain. *Erythocin* was introduced in the early 1950's and currently Abbott is the #1 generator of erythromycin in the world. The 1960's brought such products as *Selsun Blue* shampoo, *Murine* eye drops, and various infant formulas. The late nineties brought approval to use *Norvir* as an HIV and AIDS preparation, the introduction of *Gabitrol* for epilepsy and *Zemplar* for secondary hyperparathyroidism. *Flomax* (1997) is the number one product for benign prostatic hypertrophy is marketed in association with Boehringer Ingelheim. Product approvals in 2000 include *Biaxin XL, Depakote ER* and *Mobic*. In March of 2000, Abbott acquired the Knoll Pharmaceutical division of BASF. Knoll Pharmaceuticals has brought significant product additions to Abbott, adding over 2 billion dollars in annual sales with products that include *Synthroid*, a thyroid hormone, and *Meridia*, a novel anti-obesity agent. In January of 2003 the FDA approved Abbott's novel rheumatoid arthritis treatment *Humira*, previously known as D2E7. *Humira* is the first fully human monoclonal antibody for rheumatoid arthritis. Abbott currently has over 50 agents in various stages of clinical trials and has one of the largest research projects involving over 250 scientists, with Millennium Pharmaceuticals for research in obesity and diabetes.

Annual Healthcare Revenue: $16.2 billion   Ross Products $2.0 billion

Sales force: 3,200

Major Brands: *Biaxin* >$1.1 billion, antibiotic, *Depakote* antiepileptic agent, *Dilaudid, Vicoprofen* narcotic analgesics, *Ensure* nutritional supplement, *Flomax* benign prostatic hypertrophy, *Glucerna* nutritional (Ross) *Isoptin, Hytrin, Mavik* and *Tarka* hypertension, *Humira* rheumatoid arthritis, *Kaletra* HIV/AIDS, *Enfamil, Similac* infant formulas (Ross), *Meridia* obesity, *Mobic* osteoarthritis, *Omnicef* antibiotic, *Pedialyte* electrolyte formulation, *Precedex* sedative, *Rythmol* antiarythmic, *Synagis* viral prevention, *Synthroid* thyroid hormone, *TriCor* cholesterol agent, *Zemplar* bone disease, *Zyflo* asthma.

Near approval: *Atrasentan* prostate cancer, *Clivarine* deep vein thrombosis, *D2E7* additional indications, *Dilaudid CR* pain, *Hextend* hypovolemia, *Segard* sepsis, *Simdax* congestive heart failure, *Xopenex* bronchospasm.

AKZO NOBEL N.V.
ORGANON INCORPORATED
375 MOUNT PLEASANT AVENUE
WEST ORANGE, NJ 07052
973.325.4500
NASDAQ: AKZOY
ORGANON.COM

Summary: Established in 1994 Akzo Nobel operates in four different business segments, pharmaceuticals, chemicals, and coatings. The pharmaceutical division includes hormone products, central nervous system treatments, atherothrombosis treatments, contraceptives, fertility treatments, and autoimmune disease agents. The companies health-care segment includes Organon Inc. (prescription medications) Organon Teknika (hospital supplies), Intervet (veterinary products) and Diosynth (pharmaceutical raw materials). The chemical operations produce pulp and paper chemicals, base chemicals, surfactants, polymers, and catalysts. The coatings division makes paints, industrial coatings, and resins. In 2001, Organon announced moving their headquarters from the Netherlands to the United States which is the units largest market.

History: Alfred Nobel invented the blasting cap in 1863 and the beginnings of this organization. Nobel invented dynamite in 1867. The "Nobel Prize" was first distributed in 1901 (and annually since) and is named after the company's founder. The Akzo side of the company traces its origin to a German coatings developer, and a Dutch rayon maker. In 1929, these two companies merged operations creating Algemen Kunstzijde-Unie. Akzo acquired Nobel in 1995. In 1996, *Remeron* was first marketed. *Follistim* and *Mircette*, novel birth controls agent were approved in 1997. In 2001, Akzo Nobel agreed to acquire Covance Biotechnology Services, Inc. for 190 million. In addition, in 2001 the FDA approved *Nuvaring* which was launched in July of 2002.. 2002 also brought the launch of *Arixtra*. Late in 2002 Akzo announced plans to develop a male contraceptive with Schering AG.

Annual Healthcare Revenue: $3.6 billion

Sales force: 1250

Major Brands: *Antagon* hormone therapy, *Arixtra* thrombosis following surgery, *Cyclessa, Desogen/Marvelon, Gracial, Implanon, Mercilon, Mircette, Nuvaring* contraceptives, *Follistim* infertility agent, *Orgaran* thrombosis, *Remeron* depression.

Near approval: *Andriol Testocaps* male hormone replacement, *Ariza* depression, *Hextend* hypovolemia, *Implanon* a contraceptive, *Orgaran* heparin-induced thrombocytopenia, *Xyvion* estrogen agent/postmenopausal complications.

ALLERGAN, INC.
2525 DUPONT DRIVE
IRVINE, CA 92612
714.246.4500
714.246.6987
800.347.4500
NYSE:AGN
ALLERGAN. COM

Summary: Allergan, Inc. headquartered in Irvine, California, is a technology-driven, global health care company provides eye care and specialty pharmaceutical products around the globe. Allergan develops and commercializes products in the areas of eye care pharmaceutical's, ophthalmic surgical device's, contact lens care, movement disorder, and dermatologicals. Allergan research includes the areas of glaucoma and retinal disease, cataracts, dry eye, psoriasis, acne, photodamage, movement disorders, pain, metabolic disease and various types of cancer. Allergan's has been granted more than 150 patents securing its future as a specialty pharmaceutical company.

History: Founded in 1950, Allergan became a public company in 1970, merged with SmithKline Beckman in 1980, and was re-established as an independent company again in 1989. Products include eye and skin pharmaceuticals, ophthalmic surgical equipment, contact lens cleaners, and intraocular lenses. The company's skin care products include acne and psoriasis treatments. 1989 brought the approval of **Botox**. Though indicated and used to treat muscle spasms **Botox** has found wider off label usage for the treatment of skin wrinkles. 1996 brought the approval of **Alphagan**, which is now the second leading agent for the treatment of glaucoma. In 1998, Allergan added 225 scientists to its global research and development team to bring to market its specialty products. Allergan has research facilities and teams based in California, the United Kingdom, France, and Japan. **Alocril** was launched in 2000, as was the acquisition of developmental compound **Epinastine** from Boehringer Ingelhim. Also in 2000, Allergan formed a strategic alliance with eye care division of J&J, Vistakon, for research, educational efforts, marketing and co promotion. New indications for **Botox** and approval for **Lumigan** were gained in 2001. In 2002 **Botox Cosmetic**, gained approved and Allergan entered into an agreement with EntreMed Inc. to develop treatments for age-related macular degeneration (a leading cause of blindness). Currently, United States sales contribute approximately 50% of Allergan's total global revenue. Early in 2003 **Restasis** for chronic eye disease obtained FDA approval.

Annual Healthcare Revenue: $1.6 billion

Sales force: 300

Major Brands: **Alphagan, Lumigan** glaucoma, **Botox, Botox Cosmetic**, neuromuscular disorders, skin wrinkles, blepharospasm, type VII nerve disorders/cervical dystonia, **Lumigan** glaucoma, **Tazorac Gel** acne/plaque psoriasis treatment, **Restasis** chronic eye disease, **Tazorac Cream** plaque psoriasis, acne.

Near approval: **Botox** expanded indications, **Brimonidine X** glaucoma, ocular hypertension, **Epinastine** eye allergies, **Gatifloxacin** anti-infective agent, **Memantine** for retinal ganglion cells in glaucoma, **Tazorotene Oral** psoriasis, severe acne, **Vitrase** severe vitreous hemorrhage.

AMGEN INCORPORATED
ONE AMGEN CENTER DRIVE
THOUSAND OAKS, CA 91320
805.447.4587
NASDAQ: AMGN
AMGEN.COM

Summary: Currently Amgen is the world's largest biotechnology concern. Amgen develops and markets therapeutic products in four medical areas: hematopoiesis (blood cell production), inflammation and auto-immunity, neurobiology, and soft tissue repair and regeneration. Over 25% of the company's revenues are devoted towards research and development. *Epogen* and *Neupogen*, currently account for most of the company's revenue. Amgen has nearly a dozen new products under development. In addition to its own product portfolio, Amgen licenses products and technologies from and to other companies.

History: Amgen was formed as Applied Molecular Genetics in 1980 by a group of scientists to develop health care products based on molecular biological technology. In 1983 Amgen cloned the human protein erythropoietin (EPO), which stimulates red blood production in the body. The company formed a joint venture with Kirin Pharmaceuticals of Japan in 1984 to develop and market EPO. Amgen and Kirin also collaborated on recombinant human granulocyte colony stimulating factor (G-CSF), a human protein that stimulates the body's immune system to withstand bacterial infections. Amgen established a marketing arrangement with Ortho Pharmaceutical Corporation (Johnson & Johnson) in 1985 and created a link with Roche Holdings in 1988. In 1989 the FDA granted Amgen a license to produce *Epogen* (brand name of EPO) to treat anemia. The FDA granted Amgen approval to market *Neupogen* (brand name of G-CSF), to chemotherapy patients. *Neupogen* indications were broadened in 1993 to include treatment of severe chronic neutropenia (low count among certain white blood cells). In 1995 Amgen and Regeneron Pharmaceuticals declared a collaborative effort to immediately begin trials of brain-derived neurotrophic factor. In July 1999, *Epogen* was approved to treat chronic renal failure in children. In 2000 Amgen received approval for *Neupogen SingleJect*, and purchased Kinetix Pharmaceuticals in a stock transaction valued at $170 million. In 2001, *Aranesp* gained approval for anemia associated with chronic renal therapy. In July of 2002 Amgen completed the acquisition of Immunex for $16 billion, and leading product *Enbrel*. Also in 2002 *Neulasta* was launched.

Annual Healthcare Revenue: $4.0 billion

Sales force: 400

Major Brands: *Aranesp, Epogen* (*Procrit* by J&J marketed to oncology market) >$3 billion, anemia treatments, *Enbrel* >$1 billion, rheumatioid arthritis. *Kinerat* rheumatoid arthritis, *Neupogen, Neulasta* >$2 billion, recombinant human granulocyte colony-stimulating factor, as an adjunct to chemotherapy, *Neupogen SingleJect* neutropenia in HIV.

Near approval: *Enbrel* plaque psoriasis, Wegener granulomatosis ankylosign spondylitis, *KGF* oral mucositis, *LyphoCide* non-Hodgkin lymphoma, *Neupopeg* reduction in the duration of neutropenia, *Neulasta* breast cancer.

ASTRA ZENECA
1800 CONCORD PIKE
WILMINGTON, DE 19850
302.886.3000
NYSE: A
ASTRAZENECA.COM

Summary: Therapeutic arenas include anti-infectives, cardiovascular agents, gastrointestinal agents, pain control drugs, and agents for respiratory disease. Astra has research operations in Sweden, United Kingdom and United States, and subsidiaries in 40 countries. The United States is Astra's largest national market, and its United States operations embody half of a joint venture with Merck (Astra Merck). April, 1999 Astra AB and the UK's Zeneca completed their merger and Astra Zeneca was born, world headquarters based in London. Zeneca has pioneered and developed many breakthrough products including beta-blockers, anti-cancer medications, anesthetics and cardiac medications. AstraZeneca will have leading therapies in areas of gastrointestinal, anesthesia, oncology, respiratory and cardiovascular medicine.

History: Astra began in 1913 when a group of physicians and pharmacies formed the company and became its inaugural stockholders. Among this initial group of individuals was Hans Von Euler, who won the 1929 Nobel Prize in chemistry. During the 1930's research and development became the primary focus of the corporation. In the late 1940's the company began marketing *Xylocaine* (lidocaine). *Xylocaine* sales soared in the 1950's and Astra broadened production and licensing globally. Astra continued expansion through the 1970's including new leading products such as *Seloken* for heart disease. Astra paid $820 million in 1994 for a 50% interest in a joint venture with Merck to market Astra products in the United States. In 1998, Astra Merck was combined with Astra's wholly owned subsidiary Astra USA, Inc. to form Astra Pharmaceuticals L.P. Zeneca has a similar history to Astra. Zeneca has grown by bringing important new medicines to society. Zeneca has been instrumental in hormonal treatments for particular breast and prostate cancers, along with a very broad oncology line. *Atacand HCT* for the treatment of hypertension was approved in 2000. *Arimidex* for first line treatment of breast cancer was approved in late 2000. *Accolate, Atacand HCT, Nexium, Toprol XL, Entocort EC,* and *Zomig ZMT* were launched in 2001. Astra entered an agreement with E-Physician for promotion of the companies' handheld electronic prescription service. *Prilosec* is recognized as holding the position of the largest selling branded pharmaceutical in the world. In April of 2002 AstraZeneca received approval for *Faslodex* for breast cancer.

Annual Healthcare Revenue: $16.4 billion

Sales force: 6,000

Major Brands: *Atacand* hypertension, *Diprivan* anesthesia, *Entocort EC* Crohn's disease, *Faslodex* breast cancer, *Naropin* anesthesia, *Prilosec* >$6 billion, *Nexium,* >$1 billion, antipeptic ulcer agents, *Pulmicort* asthma, *Rhinocort* allergic rhinitis, *Seroquel* antipsychotic, *Xylocaine* anesthetic agent, *Accolate* asthma, *Arimidex, Casodex, Nolvadex, Tomudex, Zoladex* oncology agents, *Cefotan, Merrem* infections, *Zestril* >$1 billion, hypertension, *Zoladex* prostate cancer, *Zomig, Zomig ZMT* migraines.

Near approval: *Arimidex* breast cancer, *Casodex* early stage nonmetastatic prostate cancer, *Crestor* hypercholesterolemia, *Exanta* oral anticoagulant, *Iressa* oncology agent, *Merrem I.V.* hospital acquired pneumonia, *Naropin* pediatric pain management, *Tomudex* colorectal cancer, *Symbicort* asthma, *Zomig Nasal Spray* migraines.

AVENTIS PHARMA
ROUTE 202-206
P.O. BOX 6800
BRIDGEWATER, NJ 08807-0800
908.231.4000
NYSE: AVE

AVENTIS.COM

Summary: Aventis Pharma currently operates four business units. Aventis Pharma AG, the prescription pharmaceutical division, Aventis Pasteur, the human vaccine business, Aventis Behring the plasma protein business, and Dade Behring the diagnostic business. In June of 2002 Aventis finalized the sale of Aventis CropScience to Bayer AG. focusing primarily on the core business of pharmaceuticals. Aventis' vaccines are sold by Aventis Pasteur.

History: Founded in the mid 1800's by a chemist in the German village of Hoechst. Hoechst expanded into fibers, plastics, and petrochemicals in the 1950's. In the 1970's Hoechst acquired majority control of Roussel Uclaf of France (pharmaceuticals, perfumes). In 1987 the company purchased Celanese forming Hoechst-Celanese. In 1995 the company was renamed Hoechst Marion Roussel after the purchase of Marion Merrell Dow. Ewing Kauffman started Marion Laboratories in 1950, in Kansas City. Marion's sales in the 1970's reached $116 million; products included *Carafate, Cardizem, OS-CAL* and *Gaviscon*. In 1989 the company merged with Merrell Dow. Rorer (RPR) was created in 1990 with the combination of Rhone-Poulenc's pharmaceutical operations and the Rorer Group. In the early 1950s Rorer developed an immensely successful product that is still successful today, *Maalox*. Line extensions such as *Maalox Plus*, *Ascriptin (Maalox and aspirin)* and others helped nurture the organization. In 1995 Rhone-Poulenc purchased Fisons for $2.6 billion. Late 1999 Rhone-Poulenc SA shareholders approved their companies' merger with Germany's Hoechst AG to create Aventis SA. In 2001 Aventis entered partnership with Altana AG to develop asthma agents. Product approvals in 2001 include *BenazClin Topical Gel, Carac, Lantus, Lovenox,* and *Tripedia*. *Ketek* a new class antibiotic is expected to be launched in early 2003.

Annual Healthcare Revenue: $15.8 billion

Sales force: 5000

Major Brands: *Actonel* Paget's disease, *Allegra* >$1.5 billion, allergies, *Capaxone* multiple sclerosis, *Nasacort AQ* allergies, *Amaryl, Insuman, Lantus* diabetes, *Lovenox Arava* rheumatoid arthritis, *Azmacort* asthma, *BenazClin Topical Gel* acne, *Carac* keratoses, *Delix* antihpertensive/antianginal agents, *Cefrom, Claforan* and *Rulid* anti-infectives, *Helixate, NexGen, Kogenate FS* hemophilia A, *Ketek* antibiotic, *Lasix* edema, *Lovenox* >$1.5 billion, thrombosis, *Penlac* onychomycosis, *Synercid* pneumonia, *Taxotere* >$1.3 billion cancer, *Thymoglobulin* allograft rejection, *Trental* vascular disorders, and numerous *Vaccines*.

Near approval: *Azmacort HFA* asthma, *Dynepo* anemia due to chronic renal failure, *Exudera* (with Pfizer) short-acting inhaled insulin, *Giliadel* malignant glioma, *Hexavac* preventative vaccine, *Ketek* additional indications, *Intal HFA* bronchospasm, *Sabril* pediatric epilepsy, *Xeloda* and *Taxotere* breast cancer.

BAYER CORPORATION
400 MORGAN LANE
WEST HAVEN, CT 06516
412.394.5500
OTC: BAYZY
BAYERPHARMA-NA.COM

Summary: Bayer Corporation operates six main segments producing over 8,000 varied products. Bayer's largest segment, healthcare, accounts for one quarter of total sales through pharmaceuticals (antibiotic, anti-diabetic, cardiovascular, and hemophilia medications), over the counter medications and laboratory equipment. Other business segments are the Agriculture (animal health and crop protection), Industrial products (base chemicals, polyurethane's, solar cells), Organic chemicals (dyes, food preservatives, fragrances), and Polymers (fabrics, films, plastics, rubber). The Bayer Corporation in the United States is Bayer's largest worldwide subsidiary, accounting for about 23% of sales.

History: Friedrich Bayer established the organization in 1863. Dedication to research fueled Bayer's growth above its original synthetic dye business, leading to the introduction of such breakthrough compounds as **Bayer Aspirin** (1899) and synthetic rubber in (1915). During World War I the United States seized Bayer's American operations and trademark rights, offering them to Sterling Drug. After W.W.II Bayer promptly began rebuilding entering a joint venture with Monsanto Chemical Company (Mobay) in 1954. In 1967 Bayer purchased Monsanto's share in the organization. In the 1960's Bayer augmented its offerings in dyes, plastics, and polyurethane's, and the company built factories globally. The company grew with various acquisitions over the next 30 years including Miles Laboratories (**Alka-Seltzer, One-A-Day Vitamins**) in 1978. The company integrated its United States holdings under the name of Miles Inc. in 1992 (renamed Bayer Corporation in 1995). In 1996 Bayer introduced its first genetically engineered product, the hemophilia treatment **Kogenate**. Bayer regained American rights to the Bayer brand (known for its Aspirin trademark) and the Bayer logo in 1994 when it purchased the North American business Sterling Winthrop from SmithKline Beecham for $1 billion. Sales of antibiotic **Cipro** had reached over the $1 billion mark by 2000. During 2001, Bayer signed an agreement with Memory Pharmaceuticals to develop an agent for dementia. In 2001 **Baycol** a cholesterol agent was withdrawn from the market. Product approvals include **Avelox, Cipro I.V., Cipro Oral Suspension, Nimotop, Viadur,** and an agreement with GlaxoSmithKline, which calls for the two companies to co-promote **Vardenafil**. Early in 2003 **Cipro XR** was approved and launch of vardenafil (**Nuviva**) is expected in 2003.

Annual Healthcare Revenue: $8.8 billion

Sales force: 1300

Major Brands: **Adalat** angina, **Avelox** antiinfective, **Cipro, Cipro XL** >$1.7 billion, infections, **Kogenate** hemophilia A, **Viadur** prostate cancer.

Near approval: **Avelox I.V.** antibiotic, **Cipro OD** urinary tract infections, **Nuviva** erectile dysfunction, **Repinotan** ischemic stroke.

BERLEX LABORATORIES, INC.

SCHERING AG
340 CHANGEBRIDGE ROAD
PO BOX 1000
MONTVILLE, NJ 07045-1000
973-487-2000

NYSE: SHR

BERLEX. COM

Summary: Berlin based Schering AG product areas include prescription pharmaceuticals, diagnostic imaging agents, radiopharmaceuticals, and agricultural chemicals. Schering AG secures approximately 30% of the worlds fertility control and hormone therapy. Therapeutic areas include dermatology, diagnostic imaging, female healthcare, multiple sclerosis, therapeutics and oncology.

History: Over 20 years ago Schering AG acquired Cooper Laboratories in 1979 for entry into the United States market. North American pharmaceutical operations are under the Berlex name. Berlex is a leader in magnetic resonance imaging agents, leukemia treatment, and estrogen replacement therapy. In 1986, Berlex entered the oral contraceptive market with **Levlen** and **Tri-Levlen**. In 1990, Berlex expanded into biotechnology with acquisitions of Codon and Triton Biosciences. 1991 brought the introduction of **Betapace**. In 1993, the first interferon multiple sclerosis therapy **Betaseron** was introduced. **Climara** and **Ultravist** were launched in 1995.

1998 brought **AcuTect** and **NeoTect**, radiopharmaceuticals. The 1999 acquisition of Diatide Inc. and Oris/Cis Bio International strengthened the radiopharmaceutical therapeutic segment. In 2000 Schering AG acquired Mitsui Pharmaceuticals Inc. of Japan. Currently Schering is the world leader in contrast media marketshare. Also in 2000 **Levulan** dermatological was introduced. Product approvals in 2001 include **Campath, Yasmin, Mirena** and **Finevin**. In 2002 Schering relocated the management of the pharmaceutical division from Berlin to Montville, New Jersey and **Leukine** was purchased from Immunex.

Annual Healthcare Revenue: $4.3 billion

Sales force: 950

Major Brands: **AcuTect, Iopamiron, NeoTect, Magnevist, Feridex, Ultravist** radiopharmaceuticals for diagnostics, **Betapace** cardiovascular agent, **Betaseron** multiple sclerosis, **Fludara, Campath** oncology agents, **Climara** estrogen patch, **Finevin, Levulan** dermatology products, **Leukine** leukemia, **Mirena** intrauterine contraceptive device, **Quadramet** for cancer pain, **Levlen, Tri-Levlen, Levlite,** and **Yasmin** oral contraceptives.

Near Approval: **Angeliq, Avaden** osteoporosis, **Betaseron** additional indications, **Climara Pro** postmenopausal osteoporosis, **Endometrion** endometriosis, **Fasudil** angina, **Flucis** imaging agent, **Leukine** additional indications, **Refludan** heparin induced thrombocytopenia, **Imavist** cardiac imaging agent.

BIOVAIL CORPORATION
2488 DUNWIN DRIVE
MISSISSAUGA, ON L5L 1J9 CANADA
PHONE: (416) 285-6000
FAX: (416) 285-6499

NYSE: BVE

BIOVAIL.COM

Summary: Biovail Corporation has emerged as a full-service pharmaceutical in the United States that brings over six proprietary drug-delivery processes. Biovail applies its proprietary drug delivery technologies to successful drugs already on the market. Canadian pharmaceutical unit operates under the name, Crystaal. Chairman Eugene Melnyk owns approximately 20% of the company.

History: Since incorporation in 1977, Biovail's technologies have been used to develop 18 products, which have generated in excess of $400 million in worldwide yearly sales. The firm applies its timed-release drug-delivery systems to existing drugs that treat hypertension, asthma, and arthritis, among other disease states. Teva Pharmaceutical USA handles generic agents sales in the United States which Biovail is decreasing their presence. In 1999, Biovail announced the development of a controlled-release formulation of the anti-depressant citalopram, marketed under the trademark Celexa (Forest) in the U.S.A. 1999 also brought the acquisition of *Verelan* from Mylan Laboratories. 2000 brought the purchase of privately owned DJ Pharma in the United States, which significantly grew Biovail's United States infrastructure adding over 300 representatives. In 2001, Biovail Corporation acquired *Cardizem* from Aventis for $410 Million. Biovail also secured agreements with GlaxoSmithKline whereby Biovail has worldwide marketing rights to a once-daily version of *Wellbutrin*. Both companies will promote *Wellbutrin Once Daily* upon approval and *Wellbutrin SR* currently. Additionally, Biovail has acquired GlaxoSmithKline's *Zovirax*. Currently Biovail has over 17 products on the market in the United States, and over 20 agents in the pipeline. Biovail acquired *Teveten*, *Teveten HCT* from Solvay in 2002. In late 2002 Biovail announced that extended its agreement with GlaxoSmithKline for the marketing rights to *Zovirax* from ten to twenty years for a payment of $40 million. Also in 2002 Biovail Corp. acquired Pharma Pass LLC and its French company Pharma Pass SA for a total of $190 million. Pharma Pass Develops oral controlled release technologies and formulations.

Annual Healthcare Revenue: $309.2 million

Sales force: 600

Major Brands: *Cardizem* hypertension/angina, *Cedax* anti-infective, *Dura-vent, Rondec* allergies/decongestant, *Teveten, Teveten HCT* for hypertension, *Wellbutrin* (with GSK), depression.

Near approval: *Cardizem (R) XL,* formulations using Biovails advanced drug delivery technology including; *Buspirone* anxiety, depression/smoking cessation, *Metformin* type 2 diabetes, *Tramado* pain, *Citalopram* depression.

BOEHRINGER INGELHEIM CORPORATION
900 OLD RIDGEBURY ROAD
RIDGEFIELD, CT 06877
203.798.9988
BOEHRINGER-INGELHEIM.COM

Summary: This Ingelheim, Germany concern obtains about 85% of its net sales from prescription pharmaceuticals. The business units include human pharmaceuticals, consumer health products, animal health and contract manufacturing. Boehringer is family owned with no publicly available traded stock. The prescription business focuses on products for the respiratory, cardiovascular, gastrointestinal, rhuematology, oncology, urology, and virology therapeutic areas. Over the counter medications include the cough/cold market, analgesics, vitamin and mineral products.

History: Boehringer Ingelheim was founded in Ingelheim Rhein in 1885 where the world headquarters is still located today. The chemical business segment is the oldest of the companies units. In the 1950's Boehringer Ingelheim began its work in the animal health area. Products in this area focus on antibiotics and vaccines. In 1995 Boehringer Ingelheim acquired US company Fermenta, increasing its presence in animal care. In 1997 Boehringer acquired injectable and hospital product manufacture Ben Venue Laboratories of Bedford, Ohio and Nobl laboratories to strengthen its pharmaceutical presence. In 1997 the company launched pharmaceutical products *Mobic*, *Viramune*, *Flomax* and *Combivent*. In 1998 a new unit, Industrial Biopharmaceuticals was formed which is responsible for the contract manufacture of biotechnology products. The company is continuing research in therapeutic areas of cardiovascular, airway, and metabolic diseases. Also included are central nervous system, oncology, virology and immunological and inflammatory diseases. In March of 1998 Boehringer Ingelheim and Glaxo Wellcome PLC reached an agreement to comarket *Miracles* worldwide. In 2000, *Cafcit* received approval and Boehringer Ingelheim announced that it would provide its HIV/AIDS drug *Viramune* to developing countries free of charge. In 2001, Boehringer signed an agreement to co-market *Spriva* for chronic obstructive pulmonary disease. Products approved in 2001 include *Berodual Non-CFC MDI,* and *Micardis HCT*. In April of 2002 Boehringer Ingelheim and Shionogi & Co. established a joint venture to strengthen Boehringer's presence in the Japanese market. *Spiriva* for COPD is expected to be launched in cooperation with Pfizer in 2003.

Annual Healthcare Revenue: $6.3 billion

Sales force: 1100

Major Brands: *Atrovent*, *Combivent* bronchospasm, *Caficit* apnea in premature infants, *Aggrenox* stroke, *Catapres* hypertension, *Micardis* (with Abbott) hypertension, *Mirapex* Parkinson's Disease, *Flomax* (with Abbott) benign prostatic hypertrophy, *Mobic* (with Abbott) rheumatoid arthritis, *TNKase* acute myocardial infarction, *Viramune* HIV infections.

Near approval: *Actilyse* immediate stroke treatment, *Epinastine* ocular allergies, *Atrovent Non-CFC-MDI* bronchospasm, *Pritor HCT* hypertension, *Respimat, Sprirva* pulmonary disease/chronic obstructive pulmonary disease (COPD), *Tipranavir* HIV infection.

BRISTOL-MYERS SQUIBB COMPANY
345 PARK AVENUE
NEW YORK, NY. 10154
212.546.4000
NYSE: BMY
BMS. COM
MEADJOHNSON.COM

Summary: This New York City pharmaceutical concern established in 1989 has products in therapeutic categories that include, cardiovascular, anti-infective, anticancer, anti-AIDS, nutrition and wound care products. Bristol-Myers Squibb has increased research and development and has many new compounds in the pipeline including antihypertensive, antimigraine, and antitumor agents. Bristol-Myers Squibb is the number one producer of oncology medications in the pharmaceutical industry. In 2001, Zimmer orthopedic division was formed as an independent company and BMS acquired the holdings of DuPont Pharmaceutical Company.

History: William Bristol and John Myers founded Clinton Pharmaceutical in New York, in 1880's (renamed Bristol-Myers in 1900) to sell pharmaceuticals. Mead Johnson was purchased in 1967 (drugs, infant formula's) and Zimmer in 1972 (orthopedic products). The companies acquired several biotech concerns in 1986, Oncogen and Genetic Systems. In 1989 Bristol-Myers purchased Squibb for $12.7 billion. Fellow New Yorker Dr. Edward Squibb founded Squibb in 1850's. Developments included ether and chloroform. By the middle 1970's sales reached over $1 billion. Products such as *Capoten* and *Corgard* became market leaders among the cardiovascular segment. In 2000, BMS announced that it would divest its Clairol beauty care business and Zimmer orthopedics division to concentrate solely on the pharmaceutical segment. *Vaniqa* was approved in 2000. In 2001 BMS purchased the pharmaceutical unit of DuPont for 7.8 billion. DuPont brings key products such as *Sustiva, Coumadin*, and *Cardiolite* to the BMS portfolio. DuPont Pharma was formed in the early nineties by DuPont and Merck Pharmaceutical. Agreement was made to purchase 19.9% in IMClone Systems Inc. to develop and market oncology agents. *Estrace* a hormonal replacement therapy was sold to Galen Holdings PLC and *Clairol Beauty* division was sold to *Proctor & Gamble*. Product approvals within 2001 included *Glucophage, Glucophage XR, Levaquin* and *Videx EC.* In February 2002 approval of *Plavix* for the additional treatment of acute coronary syndrome was received.

Annual Healthcare Revenue: $19.4 billion

Sales force: 5200

Major Brands: *Avapro* hypertension, *Coumadin* venous thrombosis, *Cardiolite* radio pharmaceutical, *Innohep* deep vein thrombosis, *Levaquin* antibiotic, *Pravachol* >$2.1 billion, cholesterol agent, *Taxol* >$1 billion, *Paraplatin,* anticancer agents, *BuSpar* anxiety, *Glucophage Glucophage XR* and *Glucovance* >$2.6 billion, type II diabetes, *Videx, Zerit,* and *Sustiva* HIV products, *Tequin* respiratory infections, *Enfamil, Viactiv* nutritional products, *Plavix* >$1 billion, prevention of stroke, *Vaniqa* unwanted facial hair.

Near approval: *Aripiprazole* schizophrenia, *Atazanavir* HIB/AIDS, *Definity* contrast imaging agent, *Entecavir* hepatitis B, *Erbitux* cancer, *Glipizide* type 2 diabetes, *Garenoxacin* quinolone antibiotic, *Irbesartan* heart failure, *Vanlev* hypertension, congestive heart failure, *Zerit ER, Zerit Prolonged-Release* HIV-1 infection.

EISAI INCORPORATED
GLENPOINTE CENTRE WEST
500 FRANK W. BURR BLVD.
TEANECK, NJ 07666
201.692.7710
201.287.9050
OTC: ESALY
EISAI.COM

Summary: Eisai Co., LTD of Japan business in the United States has doubled in the past several years. Incorporated in 1941, Eisai now supports more than 7000 employees worldwide. Business segments include agrochemical products, bulk pharmaceuticals, diagnostics, vitamins, prescription pharmaceuticals, veterinary products, food additives, and a full range of pharmaceutical production equipment. Eisai now operates a global network of research facilities, manufacturing sites and marketing subsidiaries.

History: Established in 1941 in Japan, Eisai was first to synthesize and commercially produce vitamin E, along with the production of various other bulk chemicals. As recent as 1981, Eisai USA was established for chemical and pharmaceutical machinery sales. In 1995 the prescription pharmaceutical company was established in the Unites States with headquarters in New Jersey. 1997 developed and brought approval of **Aricept** (co-marketed with Pfizer), which is currently the number one prescribed Alzheimer medication in the world. 1997 Eisai Inc. opened an 85,000-square-foot, production, research and development facility in North Carolina. In 1999 Eisai's **Aciphex** was approved for marketing (co marketed with Janssen Pharmaceutica, a J&J company). Eisai and Neurogenetics Inc. announced in 2002 the extension of an agreement involving Alzheimer disease targets using human genetics. In July 2002 Eisai acquired exclusive rights to promote Pfizer's **Cerebyx**.

Annual Healthcare Revenue: $3.5 billion

Sales force: 200

Major Brands: *Aciphex* >$1 billion, ulcers, *Aricept* Alzheimer's disease, *Cerebyx* anticonvulsant.

Near approval: *Aciphex* helicobacter pylori infection, *Aricept* vascular dementia, *Cleactor* pulmonary embolism, *E2000* spasticity, muscle relaxant, *E7155* magnetic resonance imaging contrast medium, T-614 rheumatoid arthritis.

ÉLAN PHARMACEUTICALS
7475 LUSK BOULEVARD
SAN DIEGO, CA 92121
800.859.8587
NYSE: ELN
ELANPHARMACEUTICALS.COM

Summary: One of the first pure drug delivery concerns, Élan of Ireland has transformed into a fully integrated pharmaceutical researcher, developer and marketer. Products include, prescription pharmaceuticals, drug delivery systems, dermatologics, hospital products, and biotechnology products. Products in development include a vaccine (with American Home Products) for amyloid plaques characteristic of Alzheimer's disease, along with treatments for epilepsy, pain management, Parkinson's disease, and hypertension. Research facilities are in Ireland, the United States and Israel.

History: Incorporated in 1969, Élan's first product was *Tetrabid,* marketed by Organon in the United Kingdom. In 1989 Élan produced *Cardizem SR* with Élans proprietary release technology for Marion Laboratories (Aventis) of Kansas City. 1996 Élan announced the acquisition of Athena Neurosciences of San Francisco. Athena provided several agents in development for neurology in addition to a specialized neurodiagnostic testing service through its subsidiary, Athena Diagnostics. In 1998, 100 year plus Carnrick Laboratories, of New Jersey, was acquired, which included *Skelaxin.* In the same year Élan acquired Neurex Corporation, a biopharmaceutical concern. Élan purchased Dura Pharmaceuticals of San Diego to compliment its United States presence in 2000 along with the Liposome Company. In 2002 Elan put a plan to restructure its businesses, assets and balance sheet to crate a new Elan that will focus solely on neurology, pain and autoimmune diseases. In June of 2002 Elan launched *Frova*. In Juy Elan sold Athena Diagnostics Inc, as part of its recovery plan and a cost reduction that included reducing headcount by over 1000 employee's. The company is targeting to generate positive earnings by December 2003. In early 2003 Elan announced the sale of its primary care business unit to King Pharmaceuticals for $850 million, again part of its recovery plan. The transaction includes pharmaceutical products, *Sonata*, *Skelaxin* and Elan's 400 member primary care sales force. The transaction is due to be completed by the end of April.

Annual Healthcare Revenue: **$1.7 billion**

Sales force: **200**

Major Brands: *Frova* migraine, *Myobloc* cervical dystonia, *Zanaflex* spasticity, *Zonegran* epilepsy.

Near approval: *Antegren* Crohn's disease/multiple sclerosis (with Biogen), *Prialt* chronic pain.

FOREST LABORATORIES INCORPORATED
909 THIRD AVENUE
NEW YORK, NY 10022
212.421.7850
212.750.9152
800.947.5227
NYSE: FRX
FRX.COM

Summary: Based in New York City with operations throughout the United States and Europe, Forest develops and manufactures name brand, generic prescription and OTC pharmaceutical products. Forest Laboratories has subsidiaries in the United Kingdom and Ireland.

History: Incorporated in 1956 Forest products are marketed principally in the United States and western and Eastern Europe. In the United States Forest operates three sales divisions (Forest Pharmaceuticals, Forest Therapeutics, and Forest Specialty Sales). In 1984 **Aerobid** was approved for asthma. 1996 brought **Tiazac** for hypertension. In 1998 Forest Laboratories launched **Celexa**, an antidepressant that accounts for some 60% of total current sales. The company's generic products are marketed directly by its Inwood Laboratories, Inc. subsidiary. 1999, Forest promoted over 25% of their sales force due to expansion. In 2000 Forest's sales force was expanded by 70% and **Infasurf**, which treats respiratory distress syndrome in premature infants was released. Also in 2000, **Zanidip** for hypertension licensed for development from Recordati of Italy. In 2001, sales of **Celexa** grew by 67% to over $700 million. In August of 2002 **Lexapro** was approved by the FDA and December brought approval of **Lexapro Oral Solution**.

Annual Healthcare Revenue: **$1.6 billion**

Sales force: 1500

Major Brands: **Aerobid Aerospan** asthma, **Benicar** (with Sankyo) hypertension, **Celexa, Lexapro** >$1 billion depression, **Monurol** urinary tract infections, **Tiazac** hypertension, **Infasurf** respiratory distress in infants, **Cervidil** obstetrical care.

Near approval: **Acamprosate** alcohol dependence, **Lexapro** fadditional indications, **Licofelone** osteoarthritis, **Lercanidipine** hypertension, **Memantine** Alzheimer disease, neuropathic pain, **Oxycodone-Ibuprofen** narcotic analgesic.

FUJISAWA HEALTHCARE INC.
PARKWAY NORTH CENTER
3 PARKWAY N.
DEERFIELD, IL 600015-2548
847.317.8800
OTC: FJSPF
FUJISAWA.COM

Summary: Fujisawa is involved is a dynamic array of products and services, including divisions in Ethical Pharmaceuticals, Consumer Products, Medical Equipment and Supplies, Home Medical Care and Industrial chemicals. Research focuses on the areas of immunology, inflammation, cerebral metabolic diseases and anti-infectives.

History: Founded in Osaka, Japan in 1894, Fujisawa Company spans offices, plants, and research facilities in Japan, North America, Europe and Asia, and employs over 7500 individuals worldwide. Consumer Products include OTC drugs including cough, cold, gastrointestinal, analgesic and anti-inflammatory agents. Medical Equipment and Supplies segment provides many diagnostic and research reagents, including dentistry and medical checkups. Chemicals and Animal Health Products include industrial chemicals as well as antibiotic feed additives. Fujisawa established a Home Medical Care Division in Tokyo in 1995 and established it nationwide in 1996 (Japan). Fujisawa is a leading Japanese pharmaceutical concern with a history of strong research and development. Through Fujisawa's overseas subsidiaries and licensing agreements, the company is able to offer a broad range of pharmaceutical products worldwide. Currently the Ethical Pharmaceuticals division accounts for nearly 90% of total revenue. In July of 2000 Fujisawa signed a development and marketing agreement with CV Therapeutics Inc. to gain the North American rights to CVT-3146, a second-generation heart stress drug. In February 2001, Fujisawa launched **Protopic Ointment**. In April of 2002 Fujisawa and Aventis Pharma Ltd. Formed an alliance to market the injectable streptogramin antibiotic **Synercid** in Japan.

Annual Healthcare Revenue: $2.8 billion

Sales force: 175

Major Brands: *AmBisome* antifungal, *Adenoscan* cardiac imaging agent, *Cefzon* antibiotic, *Prograf* prophylaxis of organ rejection, *Protopic Ointment* dermatitis, *Rescula* glaucoma.

Near approval: *Atrisone* acne, *Micafungin* fungal infections, *Prograf* additional indications, *Protopic* atopic dermatitis in children, *Zindaclin* acne.

GENENTECH

1 DNA WAY

SOUTH SAN FRANCISCO, CA 94080

650.225.1000

NYSE: DNA

GENENTECH.COM

Summary: Genentech, Inc. is a biotechnology concern using human genetic information to manufacture and market pharmaceuticals. Genentech focuses on cardiovascular, pulmonary, oncology, and metabolic and autoimmune diseases. The company is a world leader in the manufacture of biopharmaceuticals, producing many products used for clinical research through a variety of fermentation and proprietary purification processes. , 2001 brought groundbreaking for the Founders Research Center, which will be the worlds largest biotech research facility.

History: Genentech Inc. was founded in 1976 by venture capitalist Robert A. Swanson and biochemist Herbert W. Boyer. In the early 1970's Boyer and geneticist Stanley Cohen forged a new scientific field labeled *recombinant DNA technology.* In 1978 Genentech cloned human insulin, which was licensed to Eli Lilly and Company and marketed in 1982. In 1979, human growth hormone was cloned and *Protropin* human growth hormone for children was granted approval to market. In 1986 Genentech's *alpha interferon* was licensed to Hoffmann-La Roche, Inc for treatment of hairy cell leukemia. In 1987 Genentech received approval to market *Activase*, for the treatment of blood clots in myocardial infarction patients. In 1990 Genentech and Roche Holding Ltd. of Switzerland completed a $2.1 billion merger where Roche owns 58% of Genentech's stock. Also that year the company received approval to market *Actimmune* for the treatment of chronic granulomatous disease (deficiency of the immune system). In 1993 *Nutropin* was introduced, and Factor VIII for hemophilia-A was licensed to Miles, Inc. (Bayer). *Nutropin AQ* was released in 1996. 2000 brought two new products from Genentech, *TNKase* and *Nutropin Depot*. In 2001 Genentech's approvals included *Cathlo Activase*. In April 2002, Genentech received approval for *Nutropin AQ Pen* for growth failure in pediatric patients.

Annual Healthcare Revenue: $2.2 billion

Sales force: 500

Major Brands: *Cathlo Activase* restores function to central venous catheters, *Herceptin* breast cancer, *Nutropin AQ, Nutropin Depot, Nutropin AQ Pen* and *Protropin* human growth hormone, *Activase, TNKase* myocardial infarctions/acute massive pulmonary embolism/acute ischemic stroke, *Tracleer* pulmonary arterial hypertension, *Rituxan* non-Hodgkin's lymphoma.

Near approval: *Avastin* breast cancer, *Raptiva* moderate to severe plaque psoriasis, *Tarceva* cancer, *Xolair* monoclonal antibody.

GlaxoSmithKline PLC
Five Moore Dr.,
Research Triangle Park, NC 27709
919.483.2100
NYSE: GLX
GLAXOWELLCOME.COM

Summary: As the largest based European pharmaceutical concern Glaxo SmithKline (GSK) therapeutic categories include, anesthesiology, bacterial and viral, anti-infectives, cardiology, central nervous system disorders, dermatology, gastrointestinal disorders, oncology and respiratory ailments. In December of 2000 Glaxo Wellcome and SmithKline Beecham completed a merger that would create the world's leading research-based pharmaceutical company now known as GlaxoSmithKline (GSK) based in Greenford, United Kingdom.

History: In 1873 Englishman Joseph Nathen started Glaxo in New Zealand. Nathan obtained the rights to produce powdered milk. The company went public in 1947 and Glaxo diversified in the 1950's with acquisitions of veterinary, instrument and drug distribution firms. Only in 1978, did Glaxo establish its first United States operations, which resulted in outstanding growth for the organization over the next several decades. In the 1980's Glaxo focused on its pharmaceutical segment, divesting other non-pharmaceutical operations. Glaxo launched *Zantac* in 1981. SmithKline started in 1830 as a small Philadelphia pharmacy and became a major pharmaceutical company. *Tagamet* introduced in 1976 became the worlds leading pharmaceutical product. Beecham merged with SmithKline Beckman in 1989. Thomas Beecham established an apothecary in England in 1847 and opened the world's first drug making factory in 1859. In 1995 Glaxo purchased U.K. based Burroughs Wellcome for $14.9 billion. Founded by Americans Silas Burroughs and Henry Wellcome in 1880, Burroughs Wellcome reached success with numerous antiviral agents. In 1980 Burroughs Wellcome introduced *Zovirax* and in 1987 *Retrovir*. In 1997 the FDA approved Glaxo's anti-smoking agent, *Zyban*. In 1999 Glaxo Wellcome received approval for *Relenza*, for treatment of the influenza. 2000 brought approval for *Trizivir*. In 2001 GSK signed a joint venture with Shionogi of Japan to commercialize new drugs for neurological disorders and HIV. 2001 also brought approval for *Advair Diskus, Agenerase, Rionavir, Augmentin ES, Flovent Diskus, Dutasteride, Triziver, Twinrix*, and *Ventolin HFA*. In April of 2002 GSK launched *Paxil CR*. In 2003 GlaxoSmithKline announced that it has entered an exclusive partnership with Chiron for the research, development and commercialization of obesity agents and FDA approval of *Bexxar* and *Pediarix*.

Annual Healthcare Revenue: $ 29.40 billion

Sales force: 8000

Major Brands: *Advair Diskus, Flovent* >$1.3 billion, *Serevent, Seretide, Ventolin* asthma, *Avandia* type 2 diabetes, *Amoxil, Augmentin, Augmentin ES 600* >$2 billion, antibiotics, *Bexxar* non-Hodgkin lymphoma *Ceftin, Zovirax* anti-infectives, *Coreg* hypertension/heart failure, *Dutasteride* benign prostatic hyperplasia, *Imitrex* >$1 billion, migraines, *Agenerase, Combivir, Epivir, Trizivir, Retrovir* and *Ziagen* HIV/ infections, *Paxil, Paxil CR* >$2.6 billion, depression/anxiety, *Pediarix* combination vaccine, *Relenza* influenza, *Twinrix* hepatitis vaccine, *Wellbutrin, Wellbutrin SR* depression, *Zantac* ulcers, *Zovirax, Valtrex* herpes, *Ventolin HFA* bronchospasm, *Zyban* smoking cessation, and numerous vaccine's.

Near approval: *Argatroban* thrombosis risk, *Arifo* COPD, *Augmentin XR* additional indications, *Boostrix* DTP vaccine, *Factive* antibiotic, *Hepatyrix* vaccine, hepatitis A, salmonella, *Infanrix* diphtheria, tetanus, pertussis vaccine, *Locilex* diabetic foot ulcers, *Nuviva* erectile dysfunction *Paxil CR* additional indications, *Penciclovir* herpes treatment, *Teveten* and *Hydrochlorothiazide* hypertension, *Ventolin Dry Powder Inhaler* pediatric asthma.

JOHNSON AND JOHNSON
ONE JOHNSON AND JOHNSON PLAZA
NEW BRUNSWICK, NEW JERSEY 08993
732.524.0400
NYSE: JNJ
JNJ.COM

Summary: United States based Johnson & Johnson is the largest manufacturer of health products in the world.   Pharmaceutical divisions consist of Alza, Advanced Care Products, Janssen Pharmaceutica, Johnson and Johnson-Merck (consumer pharmaceuticals), LifeScan (glucose monitoring equipment), McNeil Consumer Products Co., Ortho Biotech, Ortho Dermatological, Ortho-McNeil Pharmaceutical and Centocor. Three main segments consist of pharmaceuticals, consumer products, and professional products.

History: Brothers James and Edward Johnson founded this medical company in 1885 in New Brunswick, New Jersey. In 1886 another brother, Robert, joined to make and sell the antiseptic surgical dressings he developed. In 1897 Edward left the organization to found the drug company Mead Johnson (currently a part of Bristol-Myers Squibb). Johnson & Johnson bought gauze maker Chicopee Manufacturing in 1916. A product of Robert Johnson's dressing, the **Band-Aid** was introduced in 1921. In 1932 Robert Johnson Jr. became chairman and served until 1963. In the 1940's the divisions of Ortho (birth control products) and Ethicon (surgical sutures) were developed. In 1959 the company acquired McNeil Labs, which launched **Tylenol** in 1960. Foreign acquisitions included Belgium's Janssen and Switzerland's Cilag-Chemie during the same period.   J & J purchased Lolab Corporation, a developer of intraocular lenses used in cataract surgery in 1980, and Lifescan, a manufacturer of blood glucose monitoring in 1986. Products in the 1980's included **Acuvue**, **Retin-A,** and **Eprex**. In 1996 the company introduced **Renova** cream for use in reducing facial wrinkles and brown spots. Centocor Inc. was acquired in 1999 and in March of 2001 J&J announced the acquisition of Alza. The first transdermal contraceptive **Ortho Evra**, was approved in 2001. The FDA approved **Concerta** extended release tablets in April 2002 In July of 2002 the FDA granted approval to **Remicade** for Crohn's disease.   Early in 2003 J&J announced the acquisition of Tibotec Virco NV an antiviral treatment concern for $320 million and 3-Dimensional Pharmaceuticals for $88 million. 3DP specializes in the areas of cancer, inflammation, metabolic and cardiovascular disease. Currently J & J markets more than 90 prescription products worldwide.

Annual Healthcare Revenue: $33 billion

Sales force: 5500

Major Brands: **Aciphex** (Janssen) for ulcers, **Concerta** (McNeil) attention deficit disorder, **Ditropan XL** (Ortho Mc Neil) bladder control, **Doxil** oncology agent, **Duragesic** >$1 billion transdermal pain patch, **Floxin** >$1 billion, **Levaquin** antibiotics, **Nizoral** antifungal, **Procrit** >$3.4 billion, to reduce need for blood transfusions, **Ortho Novum, Ortho Tri-Cyclin, Ortho Evra** contraceptives, **Retin-A** acne, **ReoPro** (Centocor) cardiac ischemia, **Reminyl Oral Solution/Tablet** Alzheimer's disease, **Remicade** <$1 billion (Centocor) arthritis, Crohn's disease **Renova** (Ortho Pharmaceutical) photodamage therapy, **Risperdal** >$2 billion, schizophrenia, **Sporanox** (Janssen) antifungal, **Topamax** epilepsy, **Ultram, Ultracet** (Ortho-McNeil) pain.

Near approval: **Caelyx** breast cancer, **Dilaudid CR** pain, **Cereport** brain tumors, **Doxil** myeloma, breast cancer, **Intergel** postsurgical adhesions, **Oros Hydromorphone** chronic pain, **Ortho Elodose, Ortho Tricept** contraception, **Pennsaid** osteoarthritis, **Risperdal, Resperdal Consta** additional indications, **Topamax** additional indications, **Zarnestra** pancreatic cancer.

ELI LILLY AND COMPANY
LILLY CORPORATE CENTER
INDIANAPOLIS, IN 46285
317.277.2162
NYSE: LLY
LILLY.COM

Summary: This Indianapolis based pharmaceutical concern produces antibiotics, insulin, growth hormones, antiulcer, and cancer agents, cardiovascular products, sedatives, vitamins, and feed additives. In October of 2001, Eli Lilly announced that it would significantly expand its sales force around the globe in 2002.

History: In 1876, pharmacist, Colonel Eli Lilly, started Eli Lilly and Company. Eli Lilly died in 1898, and his son and grandsons ran the organization until the mid 1950's. Lilly introduced insulin in 1923, and blockbusters including, *Merthiolate* (an antiseptic), *Seconal* (a sedative). Lilly's pain reliever *Darvon*, at one time, was the leading prescription analgesic in the United States. In 1979 Lilly introduced the blockbuster antibiotic *Ceclor*. In 1982 Lilly introduced the first biotechnology product *Humulin*, identical to human insulin, and in 1986 introduced today's best selling antidepressant *Prozac*. In 1988 the company introduced the antiulcer medication, *Axid*. In the early 1990's the company acquired PCS Health Systems (the largest pharmaceutical benefit manager) in the United States for $4 billion. Lilly introduced *ReoPro*, a blood clot inhibitor in 1995. Recent introductions include *Humalog*, *Gemzar* for cancer and *Zyprexa*. In January of 1999 Eli Lilly completed the sale of PCS Health Systems to Rite Aid Corporation. In June of 2000, Eli Lilly announced that due to success of their product line, it was expanding the sales force. A new organization named e-Lilly was formed within the corporation to focus efforts on web-based networking with discovery partners. Eli Lilly also divested sales and marketing rights of ulcer agent *Axid* to Reliant Pharmaceuticals LLC. 2001 brought an agreement with Isis Pharmaceuticals for marketing of oncology agents under research. PDI Inc. (contract sales organization) and Lilly entered an agreement for PDI to market *Evista*. 2001 brought the introduction of *Prozac Weekly*, *Zyprexa,* and *Xigris*. Late in 2002 Eli Lilly received approval for *Forteo* for osteoporosis, and *Strattera* the first new type of medication for attention-deficit/hyperactivity disorder in over thirty years. In 2003 the FDA approved *Prozac* for use in adolescents and children.

Annual Healthcare Revenue: $11.5 billion

Sales force: 4100

Major Brands: *Actos* diabetes (with Takeda), *Evista* prevention of osteoporosis, *Gemzar* pancreatic cancer, *Humatrope* growth failure, *Humalog* insulin products, *LeukoScan* diagnosing osteomyelitis, *Prozac* >$2 billion, *Prozac Weekly* antidepressants, *ReoPro* cardiovascular agent, *Strattera* attention deficit, hyperactivity disorder, *Zyprexa, Zyprexa Zydis* >$3 billion, schizophrenia, *Xigris* severe sepsis.

Near approval: *Affinitac* nonsmall cell lung cancer, *Cialis* erectile dysfunction, *Cymbalta* depression, stress urinary incontinence, *Gemcitabine* breast, ovarian cancer, *Humalog NPL, Humalog Mix 25 HumaJect,* and *Humalog NPL* diabetes, *Olanzapine* psychosis, bipolar depression, *Raloxifene* breast cancer, coronary events, *Resiquimod* genital herpes, *Somatropin* SHOX short stature, *Zyprexa IntraMuscular* schizophrenia, bipolar mania, dementia.

MERCK AND COMPANY INC.
ONE MERCK DRIVE
WHITEHOUSE STATION
NEW JERSEY 08889-0100
908.423.1000
NYSE: MRK
MERCK.COM

Summary: This New Jersey based manufacturer is ranked as the second largest pharmaceutical company behind Glaxo Wellcome PLC. and the second largest healthcare company after Johnson & Johnson. Merck markets a broad range of human and animal health care products and services. Merck-Medco Managed Care Inc., subsidiary broker's drug purchases for managed care and employee health plans. Products include *Vasotec*, the #1 cardiovascular medication in the world, and *Zocor* and *Mevacor*, leading anti-cholesterol agents that command 40% of the market. Therapeutic areas include cardiovascular and gastrointestinal diseases, infections, ophthalmic disorders, prostate disease, and osteoporosis.

History: Theodore Weicker came to the United States from Germany in 1887 to set up an American branch of E. Merck of Germany. George Merck came in 1891 and established the firm, which imported and sold drugs and chemicals from Germany. In 1903 it opened a plant in Rahway, New Jersey. Wicker sold out to George Merck in 1904 and bought a controlling interest in competitor Squibb. During WWI Merck gave 5 billion dollars annually representing over one third of 3M's annual revenue. Pharmaceutical targeted areas by 3M are analgesics, anti-inflammatory, and cardiovascular products.

History: Minnesot*a Mining* and Manufacturing was
rmed in 1902. Early success brought such well-known products such as Scotch-brand masking tape and cellophane tape in the 1920's and 30's. The 1940's 3M brought to market the first *recor*dable magn*etic re*cordi*ng tape*. During the 1950's the company developed the Thermo-Fax copyidevelopment spending paid large dividends with *Clinoril*, *Flexeril* and *Timoptic*. In the 1980's such products as *Mevacor* and *Vasotec* were introduced. Merck purchased pharmaceutical benefit manager (PBM) Medco containment Services in the early nineties for $6.6 billion. Sales for Medco exceeded $23 billion in 2000. Product approvals in 2001 include *Cancidas*, and *Fosamax Once Weekly*. In 2003, Merck agreed to purchase the remaining 49% stake in Banyu Pharmaceutical Co. Ltd. Of Japan for $1.3 billion, establishing Merck's largest wholly owned subsidiary, outside of the United States. Merck plans to file 11 new drugs and vaccines for approval by 2006.

Annual Healthcare Revenue: $20.4 billion

Sales force: 7,000

Major Brands: *Aggrastat* angina, *Cancidas* fungal infections, *Cozaar, Hyzaar, Vasotec* >$1billion, and *Prinivil* >$1 billion, hypertension agents, *Crixivan, Stocrin* HIV/AIDS, *Fosamax Fosamax Once Weekly* >$2.6 billion, osteoporosis, *Maxalt* migraines, *Mevacor, Zocor* >$6 billion cholesterol lowering agents, *Pepcid* and *Prilosec* ulcers, *Propecia* hair loss, *Proscar* prostate enlargement, *Singulair* >$2.3 billion, number one asthma treatment in United States, *Vioxx* >$3 billion arthritis, *Zocor* >$6.6 billion cholesterol, currently the top selling drug in the world, *Cosopt and Trusopt* elevated intraocular pressure, and numerous vaccines.

Near approval: *Aprepitant* depression, *Arcoxia* for arthritis, *Cancidas* esophageal candidiasis, *Emend* for nausea and vomiting during chemotherapy, *Human Papillomavirus Vaccine* human papillomavirus infections, *Invanz* injectable antibiotic, *Pepcid* pediatric usage, *Singulair & Claritin* (with Schering Plough) allergic rhinitis/asthma, *Vioxx* additional indications, *Zetia* with *Zocor* for cholesterol, *Zoster Vaccine* prevention of herpes zoster.

Minnesota Mining and Manufacturing Company (3M)
3M Center
St. Paul, MN 55144-1000
651. 733.1110
NYSE: MMM
3M.COM

Summary: Minnesota's 3M specializes in the six segments of healthcare, specialty materials, transportation, safety, industrial and consumer goods. Healthcare products include tapes and dressings, medical and surgical supplies, pharmaceuticals, health information products and dental products. Consumer products include tapes, adhesives, office products and communication products. Transportation products include automotive components, graphics material, optical films and respirators. 3M manufacture's more than 50,000 different products and operates in more than 60 countries around the globe. The life sciences division has sales over 5 billion dollars annually representing over one third of 3M's annual revenue. Pharmaceutical targeted areas by 3M are analgesics, anti-inflammatory, and cardiovascular products.

History: Minnesota Mining and Manufacturing was formed in 1902. Early success brought such well-known products such as *Scotch*-brand masking tape and cellophane tape in the 1920's and 30's. The 1940's 3M brought to market the first recordable magnetic recording tape. During the 1950's the company developed the **Thermo-Fax** copying machine. Products that followed were carbonless papers, overheads, and numerous medical and dental applications in the 1960's. Corporate emphasis switched more during the 1970's and 80's towards healthcare. The now famous *Post-it Notes* were developed in the early 1980's. Recently in 1998 3M created the *Nexcare* brand for its line of first aid and home health products. 1999 brought 3M's drug delivery system that's delivers medications that are inhaled or absorbed through the skin, In 2000, 3M is actively seeking partners for its new pain-management programs that use transdermal and transbuccal delivery technology. 2001 brought approval of **Qvar** and 3M and Purdue Pharma LP agreed to jointly develop a transdermal delivery pain medication (patch). In April of 2002 3M sold the exclusive U.S. rights of **Qvar** to Ivax Corporation. 2002 brought expanded indications for the use of **Aldara** in patients 12 years and older.

Annual Healthcare Revenue: $3.4 billion

Sales force: 250

Major Brands: *Aerobid* asthma, **Aldara 5% Cream** an immune-response-modifier compound for genital warts.

Near approval: *Aldara* basal cell carcinoma, **Lumenax** traveler's diarrhea, **Resiquimod** genital herpes, **Neotrofin** Parkinson disease

NESTLE

ALCON LABORATORIES INC.

P.O. BOX 6600

FORT WORTH, TEXAS 76115

817.293.0450

GALDERMA LABORATORIES INC.

3000 ALTA MESA BLVD., SUITE 300

FORT WORTH, TEXAS 76163

817.263.2600

OTC: NSRGY

ALCONLABS. COM   AMEX: ACL

GALDERMA. COM

Summary: With world headquarters based in Vevey, Switzerland, Nestle is the worlds #1 food company sells more than 8,500 products in over 100 countries around the world, and has nearly 500 factories in more than 70 nations. Nestlé's five operating segments are 1) beverages, 2) milk products, nutrition and ice cream, 3) chocolate and confectionery, 4) prepared dishes, cooking aids and miscellaneous 5) pharmaceuticals. Pharmaceuticals divisions include Alcon Laboratories Inc., and Galderma Laboratories Inc. In June 2002 an initial pubic offering of Alcon Laboratories was made on the American Stock Exchange.

History: Henri Nestle purchased a Vevey, Switzerland factory that made products ranging from nut oils to rum. In 1863 Nestle was established in Switzerland. In 1867 Henri Nestle developed a powder made from cow's milk and wheat flour as a substitute for mother's milk. In 1904 Nestle began selling chocolate, and in 1929 Nestle acquired Cailler (the first company to mass-produce chocolate bars) and Swiss General (the inventor of milk chocolate). In 1938 the company introduced Nescafe, the first instant coffee. Other product introductions included Nestlé's Crunch bar in 1938, Quik drink mix 1948, and Taster's Choice coffee in 1966. Most of Nestlé's expansion took place with acquisitions in the 1970's and 1980's including Beringer Brothers wines, Stouffer, Libby, Carnation, Hills Brothers coffee, Buitoni pastas, and Butterfinger and Baby Ruth candies. Nestle first moved beyond foods in 1974 when it acquired a stake in French cosmetics company L'Oreal. Pharmaceutical company Alcon was acquired in 1977. Galderma is a joint venture formed by Nestle and L'Oreal group in 1989. In May 1998, Alcon entered a research alliance with ChiroScience Group PLC. *Loceryl* was acquired in early 1999 from Hoffmann-La Roche. *Differin* was launched in 2000. *Travatan* obtained FDA approval in 2001. In July 2002 the FDA approved *Tri-Luma*.

Annual Healthcare Revenue: $3.0 billion

Sales force: 450

Major Brands: Galderma dermatological products: *Capex* dermatitis, *Differin* topical antiacne medication, *Clindagel*, *Benzac AC*, *BenzaClin*, benoyl peroxide, *DesOwen* topical steroid, *Loceryl* nail fungus, *Metro-gel/Rozex* rosacea therapy, *Mistamine* antihistamine for urticaria. *Tri-Luma* pigment disorder.

Alcon ophthalmological products: *AcrySof* cataract surgery, *Azopt Timolol GFS* glaucoma, *Betopic, Betopic S,* intraocular pressure, *Ciloxan* ophthalmic infections, *Eye-Stream* irrigating solution, *Patanol* allergic conjunctivitis, *TobraDex* sterile ophthalmic suspension, *Travatan* elevated intraocular pressure.

Near approval: *Metvix PDT* actinic keratosis, basal cell carcinoma

NOVARTIS
556 MORRIS AVENUE
SUMMIT, NJ 07901
908.277.5293
OTC: NVTSY
US.NOVARTIS.COM

Summary: Novartis is the result of the $27 billion merger of Ciba-Geigy and Sandoz in 1996. This Basel, Switzerland-based company holds top global positions in all its core businesses: pharmaceuticals, and nutritionals. The company is also the #1 maker of chemicals for agriculture protection and the world's largest producer of jarred baby food (Gerber), and business segments in Vision, animal health, medical nutrition and health food products. The pharmaceutical division accounts for over 40% of total sales, includes products for areas as asthma, immunology, inflammatory diseases, central nervous system disorders, cardiovascular problems, endocrine and metabolic diseases, cancer and dermatology. The nutrition division is one of the world's largest providers of medical nutrition products to patients in hospitals, clinics, and nursing homes residences. Novartis has nearly doubled its United States sales force over the past three years.

History: In 1758 Johann Geigy began promotion of spices and natural dyes in Basel, Switzerland. Following generations of Geigy's continued for a century and synthetic dyes were invented in 1859. At the same time another Swiss company entered the market. Alexander Clavel joined the synthetic dye trade, forming the Gesellschaft fur Chemische Industrie (CIBA). In the early 1900's Ciba was Switzerland's #1 chemical business. Alfred Kern and Edouard Sandoz established Kern and Sandoz in 1886 in Basel also to produce dyes. Ciba, Geigy, and Sandoz were forced to compete with the Germans and the Swiss formed their own cartel Basel AG in 1918. The cartel was dissolved in 1951. All companies continued to branch out through the 1950's. Ciba and Geigy merged in 1970 and began a series of acquisitions in the United States. Ciba-Geigy entered a joint venture with biotech concern Chiron in 1986 and purchased 49% of the company in 1994. In 1996, 45 years after the breakup of Basel AG, Ciba-Geigy and Sandoz recognizing a strategic fit, reunited forming Novartis. 2000 brought the introduction of *Trileptal* and *Exelon*. In May of 2001 Novartis AG acquired a 21.3% stake in Roche Holding AG, valued at $2.79 billion and obtained approval of *Gleevec, Foradil, Starlix, Zometa*. In 2002 product approvals included *Zelnorm, Ritalin LA, Elidel Cream*, and expanded indication for *Diovan* for heart failure. Novartis increased its shareholder stake in Roche Holding AG to 32.7% and combined its 14 generic companies under one name, "Sandoz" in early 2003.

Annual Healthcare Revenue: $18.9 billion

United States Sales force: 5900

Major Brands: *Aredia* tumor induced hypercalceia, *Exelon* Alzheimer's disease, *Gleevec, Femara, Sandostatin* oncology agents, *Foradil* asthma, *Voltaren* arthritis. *Diovan* >$1.1 billion, cardiovascular agent, *Elidel Cream* atopic dermatitis, *Lotrel* and *Lotensin*, cardiovascular agents, *Lescol XL* lipid lowering agent, *Lamisil* nail fungal infections, *Miacalcin* postmenopausal osteoporosis, *Neoral* immunosupressant, *Rescula* glaucoma, *Focalin, Ritalin, Ritalin LA* attention deficit disorder, *Starlix* type 2 diabetes, *Trileptal* epilepsy, *Visudyne* macular degeneration, *Vivelle* postmenopausal osteoporosis, *Zelnorm* irritable bowel syndrome, *Zometa* hypercalcemia of malignancy.

Near approval: *Apligraf* wounds, *Cataflam* migraines, *Certican* immunosuppressant for organ rejection, *Prexige* arthritis, *Femara* breast cancer, *Foradil Certihaler* for asthma, *Letrozole* breast cancer, *Myfortic* rejection in renal transplant, *Provigil* excessive daytime sleepiness, *Visudyne* macular degeneration, *Xolair* allergic rhinitis/asthma, *Zelnorm* constipation, *Zometa* bone metastases.

NOVO NORDISK A/S

405 LEXINGTON AVENUE

STE. 6400

NEW YORK, NY 10017

212.867.0123

NYSE: NVO

NOVONORDISK.COM

Summary: This Copenhagen, Denmark-based company is the worlds leading producer of insulin. Novo's health care products account for about 75% of sales. In addition to insulin, it produces injection and monitoring systems for diabetes care. Other therapeutic segments include women's hormone replacement products, human growth hormones, and agents for depression, epilepsy and hemophilia. The company is also a world leader in the industrial enzyme market, investing heavily in the natural protein catalyst, which are often derived from microorganisms. Enzymes are developed for many uses including removing the fat out of foods to even managing toxic spills. The Novo Nordisk Foundation owns 25% of the company. Late in 2000, Novo Nordisk announced that it would separate into two independent companies, the enzymes business Novozymes A/S and health care business Novo Nordisk A/S. Over 70% of Novo's sales are diabetes product related.

History: The 1989 merger of Danish insulin producer's Novo and Nordisk formed Novo Nordisk. Engineer Harald Pedersen and brother Thorvald (a pharmacist) established Novo Industri in 1925 to manufacturer insulin and designed a syringe so that patients could administer their own injections. Within a decade Novo was in 40 countries selling insulin. During W.W.II the company produced its first enzyme, *Trypsin*, used to soften leather. In 1947 it introduced penicillin, its first product manufactured by fermentation. In the 1950's products such as *Heparin* (for blood clots). In 1982 Novo was the first to produce human insulin. By 1989 it was the worlds #2 maker of insulin (behind Eli Lilly) and the worlds largest producer of industrial enzymes. August Krogh (winner of the Nobel Prize in physiology) founded Nordisk in 1923. In 1936 the company introduced the first slow acting insulin. In 1946 the company created a new product called *NPH insulin* (protamine insulin with rapid-acting insulin), which became the leading longer-acting insulin. The 1980's brought the *Nordisk Infuser*, a pump that constantly releases small quantities of insulin. Novo produced the *NovoPen*, and injection system that resembled a fountain pen. Nordisk also developed the *Insuject pen*. After the merger Novo Nordisk introduced the *NovoLet,* the world's first prefilled disposable insulin syringe. The company introduced agents for depression, epilepsy and hemophilia in the 1990's. In 1998 Novo Nordisk and Aradigm Corporation signed an agreement to jointly develop pulmonary delivery system for administering insulin by inhalation. In 1999 *NovoSeven* was introduced. 2000 brought approval of *NovoLog,* and *Velsulin BR.* ZymoGenetics is a biopharmaceutical company spin-off of Novo Nordisk's which focus is on the discovery, development and commercialization of protein therapeutics for human diseases. In February of 2002 ZymoGenetics offered 10 million shares in an initial stock offering of which Novo Nordisk holds 39%. April of 2002 *NovoPen Junior* was approved for pediatric usage.

Annual Healthcare Revenue: $2.8 billion

Sales force: 1000

Major Brands: *NovoLog, NovoRapid* insulin product, *Norditropin Simple Xx* growth hormones, *NovaFine NovaLet, InnoLet, FlexPen, and NovoPen 3, NovoPenMate* insulin injection systems, *NovoSeven* hemophilia, *Prandin* type 2 diabetes, *Velsulin BR* DNA origin buffered regular insulin.

Near approval: *Novolin 85/15 Penfill* for diabetes mellitus, *AERx Diabetes Management System* and *Insulin Detemir* for type 1 diabetes, *Seroxat CR* premenstrual dysphonic disorder.

PFIZER INCORPORATED
235 EAST 42ND STREET
NEW YORK, NY 10017-5755
212.573.2323
NYSE: PFE
PFIZER.COM

Summary: Based in New York City Pfizer is not only the oldest American based pharmaceutical concern, but also one of the fastest growing. The combined organization is well established in pharmaceuticals, consumer health care, confectionery products, and animal medications. Acquiring Warner-Lambert in 2000, Pfizer has almost doubled its product revenue over the past several years. Pfizer Inc. and Pharmacia Corp. agreed in July of 2002 to merge in a transaction valued at $60 billion. Both companies are confident that the transaction will close near the second quarter of 2003.

History: Charles Pfizer started his operation in Brooklyn 1849. The company was incorporated in 1900 as Chas. Pfizer & Co. Pfizer was propelled into the modern drug business when the company mass-produced penicillin during the war effort in 1941. Pfizer purchased the drug maker Roerig in 1953. By the mid 1960's Pfizer had worldwide sales of over $200 million. New chairman, Edmund Pratt, increased research and development expenditures, which resulted in products such as *Minipress* 1975. Sales reached a total of $2 billion in 1977. *Feldene* arrived in 1982 and *Glucotrol* in 1984. In 1992 Pfizer released *Zoloft, Zithromax* and *Norvasc*. In 1998 Pfizer introduced *Viagra*. February of 2000 Pfizer entered into a merger agreement with Warner Lambert. William Warner opened a drugstore in the Philadelphia area in 1856. In the late 1800's he began the manufacturing of drugs by opening William R. Warner & Co. By 1945 the company had several operations around the world and acquired over 50 businesses. In 1952 Warner purchased Chilcott Labs forming Warner-Chilcott. In 1955 the company purchased Lambert Pharmaca of St. Louis and Parke-Davis of Detroit (founded in 1866) was acquired in 1970. Parke-Davis, products included *Dilantin, Benadryl* which are all still currently marketed today. In 2001 Pfizer opened its $294 million research and development campus and *Geodon* gained FDA approval. Pfizer currently has numerous brands selling in excess of $1 billion and with the addition of Pharmacia this may reach over a dozen products. 2002 brought the FDA approvals of *Bextra*, *Relpax*, *Rebif* (with Serono), *Geodon I.M.* and *Vfend.*

Annual Healthcare Revenue: $29.3 billion

Sales force: 8200

Major Brands: *Aricept* Alzheimer's disease, *Accupril, Cardura, Procardia XL* cardiovascular agents, *Diflucan, Vfend* >$1 billion antifungals, *Geodon* schizophrenia, *Bextra, Celebrex* >$2 billion, analgesic, anti-arthritic, *Femhrt* osteoporosis, *Glucotrol XL* diabetes, *Nitrostat* angina, *Lipitor* >$7 billion, cholesterol lowering agent, *Loestrin* oral contraceptive, *Neurontin* >$1.7 billion, epilepsy, post herpetic neuralgia, *Dilantin* epilepsy, *Norvasc* >$3.5 billion, cardiovascular agent, *Rebif* multiple sclerosis, *Relpax* migraine, *Viagra* >$1.7 billion, erectile dysfunction, *Viracept* HIV/AIDS, *Zithromax* >$1.5 billion antibiotic, *Zyrtec, Zyrtec-D* >$1 billion (with UCB) antihistamine/decongestant, *Zoloft* >$2.3 billion, anti-depressant.

Near approval: *Avasimibe* vascular dementia, *Capravirine* HIV infection, *Cardura XL* hypertension, benign prostatic hyperplasia, *Darifenacin* overactive bladder, *Exubera* inhaled insulin, *Lipitor/Norvasc dual therapy*, *Lasofoxifene* osteoporosis, breast cancer, *Pregabalin* epilepsy, *Spiriva* COPD, *Zithromax* additional indications.

Pharmacia Corp.
100 ROUTE 206 NORTH
PEAPACK, NJ 07977
908.901.8000
NYSE: PHA
PHARMACIA.COM

Summary: Formed by the 2000 merger of United States manufactures Upjohn, Monsanto and Pharmacia of Sweden. Therapeutic areas include oncology, central nervous system disorder drugs, anti-infectives, anti-inflammatory, and metabolic therapies. The company has two operating divisions, pharmaceuticals, which consist of prescription products for humans and animals and agricultural products, which consist of chemicals, seeds, genomics, animal productivity and nutrition research. Pfizer Inc. and Pharmacia Corp. agreed in July of 2002 to merge in a transaction valued at $60 billion. Both companies are confident that the transaction will close near the second quarter of 2003.

History: Pharmacia begun in Sweden in 1911 with products for sore throats and stomach problems. It later introduced laxatives in 1923 and vitamins in 1927 and a treatment for rheumatic diseases in 1941. Pharmacia identified a separated dextrose in 1941, and developed plasma substitute *Dextran* in 1943. By the mid 1980's Pharmacia was involved in biotechnology, health care, ophthalmology and diagnostics. A pharmacist from Indiana, Gideon Daniel Searle, formed his pharmaceutical concern in the mid 1800's. In 1890 the company was relocated to Chicago seeking improved opportunities for growth. Searle's documented first includes oral contraceptives, antiarrhythmics, anti-diarrheals, bulk laxatives, and calcium channel blockers. Dr. William Upjohn and his brothers formed the Upjohn Pill and Granuyle Company in Kalamazoo, Michigan in 1886. Products around the turn of the century were quinine, antimalarial, and the laxative *Phenolax*. In the early 1900's sales had already passed the $1 million mark. *Koapectate* was introduced in 1936. The company went public in 1958. *Motrin* was introduced in 1974. *Xanax* and *Halcion* were introduced in the early 1980's, *Rogaine* in 1988. Upjohn merged with Pharmacia in 1995 in a $6 billion deal. In 1998 Pharmacia and Upjohn announced the development of a new multimillion-dollar research center to be located in Stockholm, Sweden. 1999 brought the introduction of *Celebrex* (with Pfizer). In April of 2000, Monsanto Chemical Company (Searle) and Pharmacia and Upjohn merged to create a top-tier competitor in the global pharmaceutical industry, named Pharmacia. In April of 2000, Pharmacia received FDA approval for *Zyvox*. In 2001 gained approval to market *Axert, Azulfidine EN-Tabs, Detrol LA, Genotropin, Lunelle, Trelstar LA.* April 2002 brought the launch of *Bextra*.

Annual Healthcare Revenue: $13.8 billion

Sales force: 4,500

Major Brands: *Activella* osteoporosis, *Axert* migraines, *Aromasin, Ellence* breast cancer, *Adriamycin* oncology agent, *Arthrotec, Azulfidine EN-Tabs* juvenile rheumatoid arthritis, *Bextra, Celebrex* >$3.2 billion and *Daypro* pain and arthritis, *Camptosar* anti-cancer agent, *Depo-Provera* contraceptive, *Detrol, Detrol LA* urinary incontinence, *Genotropin* growth hormone deficiency, *Fragmin* thrombosis, *Genotropin* growth failure, *Lunelle* pregnancy prevention, *Medrol* inflammation, *Mirapex* Parkinson disease, *Rogaine* thinning hair, *Trelstar LA* prostate cancer, *Pharmorubicin* cancer, *Cleocin, Zyvox* antibiotics, *Xanax* anxiety, *Xalatan* glaucoma/ocular hypertension.

Near approval: *Benilas* rheumatoid arthritis, *Camptosar* cancer, *Celebrex* additional indications, *Deramciciane* anxiety, *Epierenone* hypertension, congestive heart failure, *Parecoxib* injectable for pain, *Roflumilast* asthma, *Somavert* acromegaly, *Thrombopoietin* thrombocytopenia, *Tifacogin* sepsis, *Vestra* depression, *Xalacom* glaucoma.

PROCTER & GAMBLE
ONE PROCTER & GAMBLE PLAZA
CINCINNATI, OH 45202
513.983.1100
NYSE: PG
PG.COM

Summary: Procter & Gamble has five main business segments. These are laundry and cleaning, paper products, beauty care, food and beverages, and health care. Products include *Tide, Cascade, Bounty, Pampers*, and *Oil of Olay, Cover Girl, Folgers, Jif, Crest*, and *Scope*. Health care is the smallest of the five business segments. In late 2000 P&G divested its over the counter acne products *Clearasil* to Boots Healthcare International and in 2001 completed the acquisition of *Clairol* beauty care business from Bristol-Myers Squibb for $5 billion.

History: William Procter and soap maker James Gamble merged their businesses in 1837 to form Procter and Gamble. By the mid 1800's Procter and Gamble had sales over 1 million dollars. Family descendants operated the company until 1930 when William Deupree became president. *Tide* detergent was introduced in 1947, and *Crest* in the mid 1950's. In 1985 Procter and Gamble pushed into the healthcare arena with the purchase of Richardson-Vicks and *Metamucil* fiber laxative from Searle. In 1996 Procter and Gamble acquired the Eagle Snacks division from brewer, Anheuser-Busch Incorporated. Procter and Gamble's over the counter segment includes *Pepto-Bismol, Vicks* cough and cold line, and *Aleve* pain reliever. Procter and Gamble pipeline includes collaborations with Alexion Pharmaceutical, Regeneron Pharmaceutical, TheraTech Inc., and AstraZeneca. 1998 brought osteoporosis agent, *Actonel*. In 2001 Proctor & Gamble announced that its health care unit was among its strongest businesses with sales up 14% over the previous year. In 2002 a once a week dosage form of *Actonel* was approved by the FDA.

Annual Healthcare Revenue: $4.9 billion

Sales force: 800

Major Brands: *Actonel* (with Aventis) post-menopausal osteoporosis, *Asacol* ulcerative colitis, *Didronel* osteoporosis, *Macrobid* urinary tract infections..

Near approval: *Actonel* osteoarthritis, *Estradiol* vasomotor symptoms in postmenopausal women, *Intrinsa* sexual dysfunction, *Pexelizumab* inflammation from bypass surgery, angioplasty, thrombolysis, and myocardial infarction, *Stedicor* arrhythmias.

HOFFMANN-LA ROCHE INC.
340 KINGSLAND ST.,
NUTLEY, NEW JERSEY 07110
973.235.5000
OTC: ROHHY
ROCHEUSA.COM

Summary: This Switzerland based pharmaceutical concern is one of the worlds largest with over 2/3 of its sales attributed to prescription medications. The Roche family has retained a controlling interest in the company since it's founding over 100 years ago. Therapeutic areas include central nervous system, infectious diseases, oncology, virology, cardiovascular diseases, inflammatory and autoimmune diseases, dermatology, metabolic disorders, and respiratory diseases.

History: Fritz Hoffmann-La Roche founded F. Hoffman-La Roche & Co. in 1896. Hoffmann sold *Thiocal* (cough medicine), *Digalen* (digitalis) and other products under the Roche name. In 1926, Roche split into two companies, F. Hoffman-La Roche and Sapac. Roche expanded and became the world's leading vitamin manufacturer. Roche continued to develop successful drugs such as *Librium* (1960) and *Valium* (1963). *Valium* was the world's best selling drug until 1981. Though now a current practice, Roche became one of the first to comarket another company's products when it agreed to copromote Glaxo's *Zantac* ulcer treatment in the United States in the early 1980's. Roche Holding was created in 1989 as a holding company for F. Hoffmann-La Roche and Sapac. The company acquired the majority stake in leading genetic engineering firm, Genentech in 1990. In 1994 Roche purchased Syntex, for $5.3 billion, solidifying its position in the North American marketplace. Roche merged its clinical laboratory operations in 1995 with National Health Laboratories, creating the world's largest clinical laboratory. 1999 brought FDA approval of *Xenical* and *Tamiflu*. Currently, Roche holds 66% of biotech concern Genentech's outstanding stock. In June 2000 Roche divested its fragrance and flavor division. Novartis AG acquired a 22.3% ownership of Roche Holding AG valued at 2.79 billion in 2001. In May of 2002 Roche agreed to collaborate with Vernalis Plc. to devlope anti depression/anxiety agents. In June 2002 approval for the merging of Chugaui Pharmaceutical Co. with Roche of Japan was obtained. In early 2003 Novartis paid an additional $2.1 billion to raise its stake in Roche to 32.7%.

Annual Healthcare Revenue: $17.2 billion

Sales force: 2100

Major Brands: *Accutane* acne, *CellCept, Zenapax* organ rejection prevention, *Cytovene, Valcyte* viral infections associated with organ transplantation, *Kytril* cancer, *Lexotan* anxiety/tension, *Madopar* Parkinson disease, *Pegasys* hepatitis C, *Rocephin* >$1 billion, anti-infective, *Roferon-A* hepatitis B and C, cancer, *Rocaltrol* osteoporosis, *Tamiflu* influenza, *Ticlid* thrombosis, *Versed* anesthesia, *Fortovase, Invirase*, *Valcyte, Viracept* HIV complications, *Xeloda, Furtulon, Herceptin Mabthera, Recormon,* and *Kytril* oncology agents, *Xenical* obesity.

Near approval: *Anti-CD 11a* psoriasis, *Boniva* postmenopausal osteoporosis, *Coreg, Dilatrend* chronic heart failure, *Fortovase, Fuzeon, Invirase* HIV, *Ibandronate* post menopausal osteoporosis, *Pegasys* addjtional indications, *Valcyte* for cytomegalovirus disease in organ transplantation, *Xeloda, Tarceva,* and *Taxotere* cancer agents, *Xenical* type 2 diabetes indication.

SANKYO PHARMA
TWO HILTON COURT
PARSIPPANY, NJ 07054
973.359.2600
SANKYOPHARMA.COM

Summary: Sankyo is Japan's second-largest pharmaceutical company (behind Takeda). Clinical, regulatory and commercial operations are based in New York, New Jersey and California. The company's research and development efforts are concentrated on allergies, antibiotics, arthritis, cancer, cardiovascular disease, diabetes, neurological agents, and obesity. Sankyo develops its drugs through an extensive independent network of laboratories in Europe, South America, and the United States. In addition to prescription pharmaceuticals, the company makes OTC medications, veterinary drugs, food ingredients, and agricultural chemicals.

History: Sankyo was established in 1899 in Japan. In 1910 a Sankyo scientist, discovers vitamin B_1. 1971 Sankyo discovered the first HMG-CoA reductase inhibitor, marking the origination of this statin class. Other discoveries included lovastatin and pravastatin. Sankyo independently markets pravastatin around the world. Pravastatin is marketed as **Pravachol** (Bristol Myers Squibb) in the United States. Sankyo is also the originator of **cefpodoxime proxetil,** a cephalosporin antibiotic sold in over 50 countries around the world. After several decades of continued growth Sankyo built the Sankyo Research Institute in San Diego and established Sankyo USA in 1985. Sanko-Parke-Davis was incorporated in 1996 and marketed the novel diabetes product **Rezulin** until its withdrawn form the market in 2000. Sankyo launched **WellChol** in the United States in 2000. In 2001 Sankyo purchased the Parke Davis share (from Warner Lambert, now Pfizer) of Sankyo-Parke-Davis. Sankyo now operates as a fully independent integrated pharmaceutical concern in the United States. Collaborations exist with Eli Lilly, Meatbases Therapeutics, X-Ceptor Therapeutics and Inceyte Genomics for bringing new therapies to market. In late 2001 Sankyo and Cygnus signed a joint promotion of the **GlucoWatch Biographer**, a device that provides glucose readings automatically and non-invasively up to three times and hour. Cygnus received approval for the **GlucoWatch G2 Biographer** in August of 2002 for children. 2002 also brought approval of Sankyo's hypertensive agent **Benicar** which is being comarketed with Forest Laboratories.

Annual Healthcare Revenue: $3.4 billion

Sales force: 500

Major Brands: **Benicar** hypertension **WelChol** lipid lowering agent, **GlucoWatch G2 Biographer** device.

Near approval: **Benicar HCT, Calblock** hypertension, **Oxytrol** urinary incontinence.

SANOFI-SYNTHELABO PHARMACEUTICALS
90 PARK AVENUE
NEW YORK, NY 10016-1301
212.551.4314
NYSE: SNY

SANOFI-SYNTHELABOUS.COM

Summary: Sanofi-Synthelabo participates in four primary disease segments, cardiovascular/thrombosis, central nervous system, oncology, and internal medicine. The combination of Sanofi and Synthelabo established in 1999 formed the second largest pharmaceutical concern in France, after Aventis. Sanofi-Synthelabo believe their $10 billion merger will move them into one of the top ten pharmaceutical companies in the United States market. Currently 88% of sales are based in Europe, Japan, and the rest of the world. Sanofi-Synthelabo has 50 new drugs (more than half in clinical trials) are in its pipeline. One of the major stockholders is cosmetic concern, L'Oreal. 2001 brought divesture of Sylachim Chemicals and Porges Urological Device's to focus on pharmaceuticals. Late in 2002 agreed to buy Bristol Myers Squibb Co's Hungarian subsidiary Pharmavit.

History: This company was developed by of an acquisition of United States based pharmaceutical concern Sterling-Winthrop in 1994 by France based Sanofi. Sanofi continued its acquisitions with acquiring Bock Pharmacal. In spring of 1999 shareholders approved a merger with Synthelabo of France. Both companies primarily participate in the same clinical areas. Of the over 20 pharmaceutical concerns in France in the early seventies, approximately 15 of them are inside the current Sanofi-Synthelabo organization. Sanofi-Synthelabo is currently the second largest pharmaceutical concern in France. *Arixtra* was launched in February in 2002 with Organon. Sanofi acquired full marketing and promotional responsibility for *Ambien* from Pharmacia in May of 2002. Oncology agents *Eligard* and *Eloxatine* was introduced in the United States in 2002.

Healthcare Revenue: $5.8 billion

Sales force: 2200

Major Brands: *Ambien* sleep disorders, *Arixtra* thrombosis after orthopedic surgery *Avapro* (with BMS) hypertension, *Eligard, Eloxatine* cancer agents, *Fraxiparine* thrombosis, *Primacor* acute congestive heart failure, *Plavix* >$1.8 billion (with BMS).

Near approval: *Dalcipran* depression, *Plenaxis* prostate cancer, *Rimonabant* obesity, *UroXatral* benign prostatic hyperplasia.

SCHERING-PLOUGH CORPORATION
ONE GIRALDA FARMS
MADISON, NEW JERSEY 07940-1010
973.822.7000
NYSE: SGP
SCHERING-PLOUGH.COM

Summary: Schering-Plough is a global leader in the areas of allergies, respiratory disorders, oncology, infectious disease, and cardiovascular disorders. The pharmaceutical division accounts for approximately 90% of the companies' sales. The company also operates in the veterinary medicine segment. Schering-Plough also includes such consumer goods as *Dr. Scholl's* foot care products, *Coppertone* sun blocks and *Afrin* nasal sprays.

History: Ernst Schering, a German chemist formed this company in the mid 1800's to provide products to pharmacists. In the mid 1900's Schering introduced *Chlor-Trimeton* (one of the first antihistamines), and the cold medicine *Coricidin* to market. In the 1960's the company introduced such novel agents as *Garamycin*, *Tinactin*, and *Afrin*. In 1971 Schering merged with Plough, Inc., of Memphis, forming Schering-Plough. *Lotrimin* was introduced in 1975, *Vaceril* in 1976, *Netromycin* in 1980, and *Proventil* in 1981, *Drixoral* nonprescription antihistamine was introduced in 1982. One of the firsts to enter the biotechnology field Schering -Plough acquired DNAX Research Institute of Palo Alto, California in 1982. Key Pharmaceuticals was acquired in 1986 and Cooper Companies in 1988. In 1993 *Claritin* was introduced and in 1994 the company received FDA approval for *Claritin-D*. Other approvals have been *Cedax*, *Uni-Dur*, and *Intron-A*. 1999 brought approval for *Temodar* for the treatment of recurrent brain cancer. *Tequin* and *Nasonex* nasal spray were introduced in early 2000. January of 2001, Schering Plough, Cor Therapeutics, and Genentech entered a collaborative agreement to promote *Integrilin* and Genentech's *TNKase* and *Activase*. In January of 2002 *Clarinex* was launched. In June of 2002 *Clarinex Reditabs* was approved. In December of 2002 *Claritin* was approved for over the counter sale.

Yearly Sales (Pharmaceutical Division): $9.8 billion

Sales force: 4,400

Major Brands: *Intron A, Peg-Intron, Rebetol, Rebetron* >$1 billion, cancer, hepatitis agents, *Integrilin* coronary syndrome, *Imdur, K-Dur, NitroDur* cardiovascular agents, *Integrilin* platelet aggregation inhibitor, *Elocon, Lotrisone* dermatologicals, *Claritin, Clarinex, Clarinex Reditabs* >$3 billion, allergies, *Nasonex, Asmanex Twisthaler, Vancenase* respiratory products, *Rebetol* chronic hepatitis C infections, *Tequin* antibiotic, *Temodar* brain tumors.

Near approval: *Caelyx* breast cancer, *Claritin* line extensions/new indications, *Loratadine* allergic rhinitis, *Peg-Intron* chronic myelogenous leukemis, *Peg-Intron Redipen* hepatitis C, *Temodar* cancer, *Vasomax* erectile dysfunction, *Zetia* (with Merck) hypercholesterolemia.

SERONO INC.
100 LONGWATER CIRCLE
NORWELL, MA 02061
781.982.9000
781.871.6754
NYSE: SRA

SERONO.COM

Summary: Swiss based Serono is the Europe's largest biotechnology concern and ranks as the worlds third largest. Serono's focus is in the three therapeutic areas of reproductive health, multiple sclerosis, and growth metabolism. Serono is the world leader in the infertility market. Serono has a presence in over 45 countries, with distribution of products in over 100 countries. Serono's genetic engineering facilities are located in the United States, Israel and Spain. The Serono Pharmaceutical Research Institute is headquartered in Switzerland.

History: Serono was originally established in 1906 in Rome, Italy under the name of Istituto Farmacologico Serono. During the war years, the company extracted insulin from beef pancreases. In the early 1960's, the first child to be conceived using infertility agent **Pergonal** was born. Expansion of the company outside Italy was started in the early 1970's with the United States operation Serono Laboratories, Inc. established to service the needs of the infertility marketplace. The mid 1970's brought expansion into Germany, Great Britain and Argentina. 1977 brought the transfer of Serono's headquarters to Switzerland. In the late 1980's Serono continued expansion into numerous international markets and 1989 the approval of **Saizen** for growth hormone deficiency, the first recombinant drug. 1996 brought the launch of **Serostim** for AIDS wasting. In 1997 **Gonal-F** was approved and in 1998 Geneva Medical Research Institute was acquired from Glaxo-Wellcome. 2000 brought approval for **Ovidrel**, and the acquisition of **Cetrotide** from ASTA Medica. **Ovidrel** and **Cetrotide** were launched in 2001. **Rebif** for multiple sclerosis was launched in 2002 with compromotion partner Pfizer. In 2002 Serono acquired Genset to further develop drug discovery. **SeroJet** was introduced in February of 2002. Currently Serono has six recombinant products on the market.

Yearly Sales: $1.3 billion

Sales force: 200

Major Brands: *Cetrotide, Metrodin HP, Pergonal, Profasi, Luveris,* and *Ovidrel* infertility treatments, *Crinone* progesterone gel, *Gonal-F, Gonal F Multi-Dose* ovulation disorders, *Rebif* multiple sclerosis, *Saizen* growth hormones, *Serostim* AID's wasting, *Serophene* ovulatory failure, *Stilamin* esophageal varices, *SeroJet* needle free drug delivery systems.

Near Approval: *Lutropin Alfa* female infertility, *r-FSH Improved Formulation* fertility, *Serostim* HIV symptoms, short bowel syndrome.

SOLVAY AMERICA INC.
901 SAWYER ROAD
MARIETTA, GA 30062
770.578.9000
OTC: SVYSY
SOLVAYPHARMACEUTICALS-US. COM

Summary: Solvay is based in Brussels, Belgium and is the largest chemicals operation in the country. Solvay produces numerous plastic compounds for construction and auto industries. Solvay' customers are manufacturers and commercial businesses operating in areas of construction, consumer and capital goods and services sectors. Plastics account for more than half of the corporation's revenue. The pharmaceutical division accounts for 25% of Solvay's total revenue. In the United States the company operates through Solvay Pharmaceuticals, Inc.

History: Ernest Solvay discovered Solvay in 1863. Solvay had developed a unique process for producing sodium carbonate (soda ash). In the late 1800's Solvay had soda ash plants in most of Europe and became the world's leading producer. In the 1950's Solvay started selling polyvinyl chloride (PVC) and in the 1970's a range of polypropylene products including automobile parts, pipes and interior decoration goods. In 1980 Solvay with its experience in organic chemistry set up a separate health sector. Solvay acquired various pharmaceutical concerns including Kali-Chemie (Germany), Latema, and Sarbach (France) Duphar (Netherlands) and Reid-Rowell (USA) in 1986 (presently Solvay Pharmaceuticals Inc., USA). In June of 1999 Solvay Pharmaceuticals Inc. agreed to acquire Unimed Pharmaceuticals Inc. of Chicago in a deal valued at over $123 million. Also in 1999 Solvay acquired hypertension products **Aceon** from Servier SA of France. Solvay markets **Estratest** and **Prometrium** with Duramed in the United States. **AndroGel** was approved in spring of 2000 to treat male hypogonadism. 2000 also brought the acquisition of Sintofarma Pharmaceuticals of Brazil. 2001 brought **Marinol** (from Roxane Laboratories). Solvay agreed to sell U.S. marketing rights for **Teveten** and **Teveten HCT** in March of 2002 to Biovail Corporation.

Healthcare Revenue: $1.5 billion

Sales force: 1000

Major Brands: **Aceon** hypertension, **AndroGel** (with TAP) testosterone deficiency, **Cenestin** menopause, **Creon** pancreatic deficiencies, **Estratest, Estratab** estrogen replacement therapy, **Lithobid** manic depressive illness. **Marinol** appetite stimulant, **Prometrium** oral progesterone, **Physiotens** hypertension.

Near approval: **Anoheal,** anal fissures, **Incostop** incontinence, **Cilansetron** irritable bowel syndrome, **Estratest** expanded indications, **Estrogel** estrogen replacement therapy, **Fluvoxamine** obsessive compulsive disorder, **Tedisamil** arrhythmia's, **Omacor** secondary prevention of myocardial infarction.

TAKEDA PHARMACEUTICALS NORTH AMERICA, INC.
MILLBROOK BUSINESS CENTER
475 HALF DAY ROAD, SUITE 500
LINCOLNSHIRE, ILLINOIS 60069
847.383.3000
OTC: TDCHF

TAKEDAPHARM.COM

Summary: Japan's top drug maker, Takeda Chemical Industries Ltd., makes and markets pharmaceuticals, vitamins, food additives, bulk vitamins and chemical products. Areas of research and development include treatments for ulcers, prostate cancer, hypertension, and diabetes. Development partners include Novo Nordisk, and Celera Genomics. German firm BASF and Takeda have combined their bulk vitamin operations in the United States.

History: Over two centuries ago in 1781, 32-year-old Chobei Takeda I started a business selling traditional Japanese and Chinese medicines in Doshomachi, Osaka. In 1895, the Company established its own factory and became a pharmaceutical manufacturer. Takeda began direct imports from England, the U.S., Germany, Spain and other countries around 1895, and in 1907 obtained exclusive sales rights in Japan for products from German company Bayer. During the late 1940's Takeda produced antibiotics, cardiac agents, and vitamins. In 1950 Takeda launched the first multivitamin in Japan. Takeda steadily expanded its pharmaceutical business and even began exports to the United States, Russia and China. The 1960's brought expansion into Asia, and the 1970's brought expansion into Europe. In 1985 Takeda first enters the United States market by forming TAP Pharmaceuticals Inc. (now TAP Pharmaceutical Products Inc.) in the U.S. in a 50:50 joint venture with Abbott Laboratories. TAP began marketing *Lupron* in the same year, followed by *Lupron Depot* in 1989, and *Prevacid* in 1995. Established in 1998, Takeda Pharmaceuticals North America was created to take advantage of Takeda Chemical Industries' growing, international pharmaceutical presence. *Actos* was launched as Takeda Pharmaceutical North America's first product. Late in 2000, Takeda announced that it has formed Takeda Research Investment for equity investment into biotechnology ventures with research targets or technologies for innovative pharmaceutical discoveries. In April of 2002 *Prevacid* reached the number one prescribed proton pump inhibitor in the United States.

Annual Healthcare Revenue: $6.9 billion

Sales force: 1000

Major Brands: *Actos* <$1 billion (with Eli Lilly) type 2 diabetes, *Atacand* (marketed by AstraZeneca) hypertension, *Lupron*, *Lupron Depot* >$1 billion (marketed by TAP) prostate cancer, *Prevacid* (marketed by TAP) >$3 billion, ulcer treatment.

Near approval: *Biopress* heart failure, *Prevacid* additional indications, *Risedronate Sodium* osteoporosis, *Apomorphine* erectile dysfunction

WYETH PHARMACEUTICALS
5 GIRALDA FARMS
MADISON, N.J. 07940
973.660.5000
NYSE: WYE
WYETH.COM

Summary: This diversified chemical maker's products include pharmaceuticals, consumer health products, herbicides, veterinary products, and human vaccines. Subsidiaries include Wyeth Pharmaceuticls. , Wyeth Consumer Healthcare (over the counter pharmaceuticals), Fort Dodge Animal Health (veterinary products). Pharmaceutical division Wyeth Pharmaceuticals focuses on woman's health, infant nutritionals, cardiovascular, neuroscience therapies, gastroenterology, anti-infectives, vaccines, oncology and musculoskeletal therapies.

History: Established in 1926, American Home Products acquired over 30 food and drug companies through the depression (including John Wyeth and Brother) increasing its size dramatically. *Preparation H*, was a sunburn treatment acquired in 1935. *Anacin* was also procured around the same period. Canadian company Ayerst Laboratories (*Premarin*) was acquired in 1943. Ayerst developed *Inderal* in 1968. Acquisitions continued with the acquisition of Bristol-Myers animal health division 1983, and A.H. Robins in 1988. In 1994, American Home Products purchased American Cyanamid (Lederle) for a reported price of $9.6 billion. In 1948, Lederle discovered the antibiotic chlortetracycline (*Aureomycin*.) American Home Products introduced various new products in the United States including in 1996, the antidepressant *Effexor*. 1997 brought *Lodine XL* and *Prempro*. 1999 brought *Enbrel* a disease modifying rheumatoid arthritis agent, *Meningitect* a vaccine for meningococcal group C disease and *Rapamune* for prevention of organ transplants. 2000 products include, *Mylotarg, ReFacto, Prevnar,* and *Protonix* and the sales of Cyanamid agricultural division to BASF. In 2001, AHP obtained approval of *Effexor XL* for general anxiety disorder and prevention of depressive disorder relapse. Also AHP formed *Wyeth Women's Healthcare* as global business unit within Wyeth-Ayerst Pharmaceuticals. Product and expanded indications for 2001 include, *Protonix Tablet, Protonix I.V.,*and *Rapamune Tablet.* In 2002 American Home Products changed the name of their organization to Wyeth, paying tribute to one of the company's oldest prescription medicine business and founder John Wyeth.

Annual Healthcare Revenue: $14.1 billion

Sales force: 4,400

Major Brands: *Altace* (with King Pharmaceuticals) hypertension, *Cordarone I.V.* arrhythmias, *LoOvral, Min-Ovral, Nordette* and *Triphasil* oral contraceptives, *Effexor, Effexor XR* >$1.5 billion, antidepressant/anxiety, *Enbrel* (with Amgen) rheumatoid arthritis, *FluShield* influenza virus vaccine, *Rapamune* prevention of organ rejection, *Mylotarg, Neumega* oncology agents, *Novatrone* multiple sclerosis, *Premarin, Prempro, Premphase* >$2 billion, hormonal replacement, *Prevnar* >$1 billion, pneumococcal disease vaccine, *Protonix, Protonix I.V.* ulcers/heartburn, *Rapamune* organ rejection, *ReFacto* hemophilia, *Zosyn* anti-infective, *Ziac* hypertension and numerous *Vaccines*.

Near approval: *Alesse* acne, *Effexor XL* additional indications, *Flu Mist* influenza, *InFuse Bone Graft* acute long bone fractures, *ReFacto AF* hemophilia, *Premarin Low Dose* hormonal replacement.

CONTACT SALES ORGANIZATIONS

Contract sales organizations (CSO's) are well established in the pharmaceutical sales channel. The utilization of CSO's is widely recognized as a solid business strategy, one that plugs in trained professionals that can be integrated or act alone offering maximum agility and effectiveness. Contracts can range to tempory fill-ins while a representative is out of a territory to contracts of two to three years in duration. Often contracts will provide an option clause by which the traditional pharmaceutical concern has the opportunity to adopt the CSO representatives into their own company's sales force. CSO's are a cost effective, efficient marketing strategy. CSO's possess a strong stable of experienced pharmaceutical reserves that are waiting to be called into action. CSO's may have up to 300 representatives ready to meet any manufactures needs quickly and efficiently. Some needs that CSO's meet in the marketplace:

• Traditional pharmaceutical companies need to increase their sales force for a successful product launch

• Rx prescription drugs are shifting to over-the-counter status that requires a separate sales force

• An emerging, foreign, or start up pharmaceutical/biotech company who does not possess the infrastructure and competencies by which to manage a sales force in the United States

• Regional business strategies to meet specific segments in the industry, such as:
   managed care pull-though strategies, long term care, retail pharmacies, distribution

• A mature product that has not received appropriate promotional attention

• Staffing for convention exhibits, trade shows, medical conferences to keep from pulling staff from their territories

• Providing mirror territories to the traditional pharmaceutical company increasing reach, frequency, and voice in the marketplace

As with any sales position, CSO's like any of us, are held to reaching their numbers. Contracts include measurement tools by which to assess the contribution made by the CSO.

Candidates find that CSO's provide for an excellent entry to the pharmaceutical industry, or a graceful exit. Candidates are interviewed in the same manner as traditional pharmaceutical companies, with the same requirements and competency expectations. CSO's may be more relaxed in the necessity of a four-year degree with those candidates that are registered nurses (with A.A. degree's or diploma programs). CSO's also offer increased flexibility to many individuals with both full and part time employment. Career paths for sales management and sales training are similar to those of traditional pharmaceutical concerns. Marketing careers are limited by the nature of the CSO business (no ownership of specific products).

Imagine the impact and knowledge delivered by a 30-year pharmaceutical sales veteran who now has decided to cut back to 20 hours a week in semi-retirement; the rapport he has established with his a clientele may even open new doors for the CSO. The flexibility of a part-time job for the working mother as she sets her own hours during the workweek to continue her professional career is also a benefit. This helps fill the large void in the United States.

CSO's do not want to be the "minor league" of the pharma industry. Representatives are compensated by a base salary and commission, or may be paid by the number of sales calls. Total compensation packages have been traditionally less than full time positions, but this gap has closed in recent years.

Their training is similar to full time sales professionals. Sound business decisions and excellent customer needs are paramount, perhaps requiring adjusting their territories to fit their timeframe. The physicians' needs for continuing education must be met; the days of leaving brochures and samples are gone. These Representatives must be able to sell, and close the sale. Some CSO's have their own training departments, while others use the contracting company's training programs. As with traditional companies, training consists of home study, significant classroom time, product knowledge, and selling skills.

Physicians, pharmacists, and managed care institutions are unaware that they are interfacing with a CSO Representative. All sales material, literature, samples, and business cards are provided by the traditional pharmaceutical company under contract. At other times, a small designation of the CSO is listed on the Representative's business card. Unlike the *Insight* strategy for networking with traditional Pharma companies, *Insight* recommends making direct contact with these organizations through their websites. Listed below is a sampling of some of the major contract sales organizations.

DENDRITE INTERNATIONAL, INC.
1200 MT. KEMBLE AVENUE
MORRISTOWN, NJ 07960
973.425.1200
973.425.2100
DENDRITE.COM

VENTIV HEALTH U.S. SALES
200 COTTONTAIL LANE
SOMERSET NJ 08873
800.390.5003
800.228.4343
212.768.8000
VENTIV.COM

INNOVEX INC.
WATERVIEW CORPORATE CENTRE
10 WATERVIEW BLVD
PARSIPPANY, NJ 07054
800.605.3230
973.257.4500
INTERVIEW WITH THE INTERACTIVE VOICE RESPONSE (IVR) SYSTEM, USE REFERENCE NUMBER 1234
INNOVEXGLOBAL.COM

McKesson Pharmaceutical Partners

101 COLLEGE ROAD EAST
PRINCETON, NJ 08540
609.919.3900
609.919.3931
MCKHBOC-PPG.COM

Nelson Professional Sales

2000 LENOX DRIVE, SUITE 100
LAWRENCEVILLE, NJ 08648
609.896.4712
800.672.0676
NELSONPROFESSIONALSALES.COM

Professional Detailing Incorporated (PDI)

10 MOUNTAINVIEW ROAD, SUITE C200
UPPER SADDLE RIVER, NJ 07458
800.242.7494
PDI-INC.COM

ATTACH BUSINESS CARDS HERE	ATTACH BUSINESS CARDS HERE

DATES AND NOTES FROM TELEPHONE CONTACTS:

CURRENT/FUTURE JOB OPPORTUNITIES:

DISTRICT MANAGER NAME, ADDRESS, PHONE:

PRECEPTORSHIP SCHEDULING:

ADDITIONAL PROFILE AND CONTACT INFORMATION:

ATTACH BUSINESS CARDS HERE	ATTACH BUSINESS CARDS HERE

DATES AND NOTES FROM TELEPHONE CONTACTS:

CURRENT/FUTURE JOB OPPORTUNITIES:

DISTRICT MANAGER NAME, ADDRESS, PHONE:

PRECEPTORSHIP SCHEDULING:

ADDITIONAL PROFILE AND CONTACT INFORMATION:

DATES AND NOTES FROM TELEPHONE CONTACTS:

CURRENT/FUTURE JOB OPPORTUNITIES:

DISTRICT MANAGER NAME, ADDRESS, PHONE:

PRECEPTORSHIP SCHEDULING:

ADDITIONAL PROFILE AND CONTACT INFORMATION:

139

ATTACH BUSINESS CARDS HERE	ATTACH BUSINESS CARDS HERE

DATES AND NOTES FROM TELEPHONE CONTACTS:

CURRENT/FUTURE JOB OPPORTUNITIES:

DISTRICT MANAGER NAME, ADDRESS, PHONE:

PRECEPTORSHIP SCHEDULING:

ADDITIONAL PROFILE AND CONTACT INFORMATION: